"*The Beautiful Wife* is a practical, catch-all book for women who want to explore and discuss what it means to be married in every sense of the term. Sandy Ralya covers everything. Chapter 7, on communication, is worth the price of the book in itself—one of the best discussions I've read on that topic."

—GARY THOMAS,
author of *Sacred Marriage* and *A Lifelong Love*

"What started as a popular mentoring program is now an incredible handbook that every woman needs. I believe this book will be life-changing for many, many women and their marriages."

—SHAUNTI FELDHAHN,
best-selling author of *For Women Only*

"Sandy Ralya candidly shares her experiences, others' personal stories, and God's wisdom to mentor women for great marriages."

—FLORENCE LITTAUER,
speaker and best-selling author of *Personality Plus*

"Simply and honestly, Sandy speaks to the real issues that wives deal with and gives practical guidance on how to become 'beautiful' in Christ."

—DAN SEABORN,
author and founder of Winning at Home

D0187697

Expand your journey through *The Beautiful Wife*
with these other resources by Sandy Ralya

The Beautiful Wife Prayer Journal
The Beautiful Wife Mentor's Guide

the Beautiful wife

Focused on Christ, Fulfilled in Marriage

Sandy Ralya

Kregel Publications

For Deb, Suzann, and Nancy—
the community of women who've mentored me
from my earliest days as a wife
I'm grateful for your love, wisdom, and grace.

Contents

Acknowledgments	9
How to Use This Book	13
Introduction	17
1. Equipping for the Journey	19
2. Attending to Self-Care	41
3. Living as the Genuine Article	57
4. Cultivating Mystique	71
5. Inviting Romance	89
6. Thinking Differently About Sex	107
7. Opening Lines of Communication	127
8. Speaking Truth in Love	141
9. Managing Money	163
10. Creating a Culture of Beauty	181
11. Professionalizing the Roles of Wife and Mother	199
12. Choosing God's Best	217
What's Next?	223
Appendix: Resources for Continued Growth	225
Notes	231
About Sandy Ralya and Beautiful Womanhood	237

Acknowledgments

My Lord and Savior Jesus Christ: Each new day, You wait longingly for my first glance in Your direction—I love the way You love me! It fills me like nothing and no one else can. Thank You for pouring out Your life for me, offering proof I was worth dying for. I am a beautiful wife because of Your redeeming work.

Tommy B.: You have blessed the ministry of Beautiful Womanhood! When our youngest entered high school and I announced I wanted to learn to improve my speaking skills, you sent me to speaker's school. Speaking led to writing. Writing led to my passion for mentoring. And the rest, as they say, is history. Once I began this book, you called me an author. You listened to countless outlines forming in my head and spilling out of my mouth. You fixed my laptop, served me lattes, provided fun, and told anyone willing to listen that I was writing a book. Yes, your fingerprints are all over the Beautiful Womanhood ministry and *The Beautiful Wife*. Thanks for letting me share our story. You may never know (this side of heaven) how many women have been blessed as a result. I love you!

Stacy Bajema: From the day I mouthed the words, "I need your help birthing this book," you took on the role with fervor and strength. We've come a long way from the days of poring over whiteboards at the lake and I treasure each step we took. This book would not have been written without the sacrifices you and Mark made. My gratitude, love, and respect for you are enormous!

Suzann VanKlompenberg: It's hard to put into words what your friendship has meant to me throughout the years. When you wrote, "Our friendship won't end unless you choose to walk away," wounds inflicted in childhood began healing. Thanks for teaching me what true friendship is. I learn much by listening to and watching you. Most recently, you have challenged me to be what was sometimes painfully honest, to go deeper than a superficial level as I wrote this book. My readers and I owe you a debt of gratitude for your persistence. Your contributions to the Beautiful Womanhood ministry have been invaluable. I love you, dear friend.

Cat Hoort, trade marketing and publicity manager at Kregel Publications: Though we'd only met twice, you quickly caught my vision for the ministry potential *The Beautiful Wife* and its companion books could have in the lives of women. God answered many prayers through your belief and I'm grateful. Numerous women will benefit from small group community because of your investment in this project.

Dawn Anderson, editor at Kregel Publications: There's no denying you're a skilled editor; yet I'm even more impressed by your ability to listen to and obey the voice of the Holy Spirit. Your contributions to this book hold the potential to cause increased fruit in each reader's life. I've loved working with you and, as always, you're safe on a soapbox with me! God bless you!

Angela Pleune: Thank you for contributing the hostess chapter for *The Beautiful Wife Mentor's Guide*. With so many mentors requesting that chapter, your willingness to take on this task was a particular blessing. I can't think of anyone more suited to share the instructional wisdom behind the gift of hospitality, as I've been the fortunate recipient of many a splendid hour around your table.

Bill and Dena Curnow: Though I didn't want to hear it at the time, you were right. Beautiful Womanhood could be expanded to meet the needs of more women than I first imagined. Thanks for sharing your wisdom and avoiding the temptation to gloat!

Dorie Meendering: Your ability to listen and your willingness to wait on the Lord gave Beautiful Womanhood small groups an opportunity to exercise their newfound wings in our church. Your encouragement cheered me, your wisdom helped guide me, and your mentorship prepared me to lead. Many thanks, dear teacher!

Susan Hegel and Ridge Point Community Church: Thanks for your perseverance and grace while using the Beautiful Womanhood program in its fledgling state. Your feedback helped shape this book.

How to Use This Book

SMALL GROUP USE

Ideally, *The Beautiful Wife*— and its companion books—can be used as the curriculum for a Beautiful Womanhood small group. In these groups, a mentor (or co-mentoring pair) gathers with up to six other wives to discuss the Reflection questions following each chapter of *The Beautiful Wife* and to hold each other accountable to take the First Steps toward change.

Beautiful Womanhood groups can originate in your church. (To help you get started, there is a free small-group starter kit available on the churches/ministries page at www.beautifulwomanhood.com.) Or you might gather informally with friends and neighbors to form a group. If you are not able to form a Beautiful Womanhood small group at this time, you can contact info@beautifulwomanhood.com to see if there are groups already meeting in your area that you might be able to join.

INDIVIDUAL USE

Although a small group setting is the ideal way to grow with *The Beautiful Wife*, it can also be used individually. After reading each chapter, write down your responses to the Reflection questions and take the First Steps listed. If you are able to find one other wife to read through the book at the same time, you can encourage one another.

To enrich your journey, I recommend you also use *The Beautiful Wife Prayer Journal*, described below. Also, be sure to join in on conversations with other wives reading *The Beautiful Wife* via the Beautiful Womanhood page on Facebook (www.facebook.com/BeautifulWomanhood). For ongoing marriage enrichment, I encourage you to subscribe to my blog at www.beautifulwomanhood.com/blog.

Special Note

The Beautiful Wife is for marriage enrichment. If you are dealing with serious marriage issues such as infidelity or addictions, you should seek professional help, knowing that God loves you and desires your healing and protection. If you are in a physically or emotionally abusive relationship, it is not your fault! Please seek help and safety immediately by contacting a pastor, trained Christian counselor, or the domestic abuse hotline at 1-800-799-SAFE (7233).

COMPANION MATERIALS

Prayer Journal

For additional marriage enrichment, *The Beautiful Wife Prayer Journal* corresponds to each chapter in *The Beautiful Wife*. In this journal you'll find:

+ Prayers for each topic with a place to journal any inspiration or challenges the prayer evokes
+ Space to journal prayers in response to relevant Scripture verses, and to fashion Scripture into prayers to pray for you, your husband, and your marriage

+ Opportunities to record prayer requests and answers for you and your husband
+ Prompts that lead you to reflect, set goals, and envision change

After chronicling your journey through twelve chapters in *The Beautiful Wife Prayer Journal,* refer back to it throughout the life of your marriage. Doing so will prevent a lot of aimless wandering as you regularly refresh your understanding of all you learned from this study.

Mentor's Guide

The Beautiful Wife Mentor's Guide includes everything a mentor needs to begin leading a Beautiful Womanhood small group:

+ A short introduction on what it means to be a mentor
+ Instructions on how to create a group, get a mentoring ministry started, and how to get your church involved
+ Practical tips for mentoring a small group
+ A hostess guide
+ A week-by-week leader's guide that corresponds with each chapter of *The Beautiful Wife*

Mentors can find additional help and resources online with pages specifically for mentors. Go to www.beautifulwomanhood.com and www.facebook.com/BeautifulWomanhoodMentors.

Introduction

*D*on't let the title confuse you. This isn't a book for women pursuing physical beauty or perfection as defined by our culture. *The Beautiful Wife* is a book for the gloriously messy woman who has serious and not-so-serious questions about her role as a wife. It's a book for the woman who longs to develop deep relationships with real women who don't gloss over the dirty realities of life. It's a book for the woman who wants to experience more fulfillment, passion, and meaning in her marriage.

It is my desire to help women focus on God through all the hills and valleys of marriage, just as other women have helped and continue to help me. I've mentored women one-on-one, taught marriage-focused Bible studies, led women's marriage seminars, and I founded the marriage mentoring ministry called Beautiful Womanhood, which I currently direct. This book grew from all of those experiences. Join me as I share biblical principles and their practical application, illustrating them with real-life experiences.

In this day and age, it can be difficult to understand the role of a wife. As a matter of fact, it's always been a hard role to understand; it's just not a one-size-fits-all kind of job. Your marriage is different from mine, and both of our marriages are different from your friend's. And even after you've settled into it, the role requires tweaking with each new season of life. Getting recipe theology—a cookie-cutter formula—in response to our marriage questions leaves us hungry. But there are relevant biblical answers that satisfy.

As you journey through the twelve chapters in *The Beautiful Wife*, I believe you'll find some of those answers. In fact, the more you turn to God and talk vulnerably within a loving community of women, the more answers you'll find. When women share with each other the details of their journeys with God as wives, it's a beautiful thing indeed. I believe the stories of imperfect women with imperfect marriages will refresh you and also challenge you to make changes in your role as a wife, which will improve your marriage. That is my prayer for you—that through personal change your marriage will be transformed too!

CHAPTER ONE

Equipping for the Journey

❧

Make me walk along the path of your commands,
for that is where my happiness is found.

—PSALM 119:35

As you follow Me, I lead you along paths of newness:
ways you have never imagined. Don't worry about what
is on the road up ahead. I want you to find your security
in knowing Me, the One who died to set you free.

—SARAH YOUNG, *JESUS CALLING*

When I met Tom, he swept me off my feet, and I eagerly agreed to be his wife. Throughout our short engagement, I observed things in him that concerned me, but I overlooked them—I was getting married! We could work on the rough edges later. On a cold December day, Tom and I passionately vowed our lives to one another forever.

It wasn't winter's icy winds that cooled my passion to love, honor, and cherish. It was my inability to deal with Tom's rough edges grating on my own. Marriage is all about becoming one, and I had no idea how to make that happen. I needed help.

I had heard good teaching at church, but I didn't understand how to make the information practical and relevant to my situation. I was afraid to talk about my marriage and expose its rotten spots; everyone else's marriage seemed so good. Ill-equipped and isolated, I responded to my marriage problems with what came naturally to me: preaching at Tom. When preaching didn't work, I got angry or withdrew my love to signal my hurt or disappointment. That didn't work either, and it made us both miserable.

After eleven years of suffering, I decided there had to be a better way of dealing with the problems I faced rather than simply protecting myself from getting hurt or retaliating in anger. I turned toward God and began studying His Word. I also revealed my secret pain to others. God used His Word and wise women—friends, family members, and a Christian counselor—to mentor me, which enlarged my understanding of my role as a wife. As I learned and grew, I made choices to reverse negative cycles that had plagued me for years. When I gave God the control over my marriage relationship, He accomplished in five months what I couldn't in eleven years. He turned our marriage around and began the process of healing it.

Who can you turn to when you're struggling with marriage issues? Where do you find the practical advice you need to make a good marriage great? What is God's truth concerning your role as a wife?

My experience parallels a biblical plan for strengthening marriages. In Paul's letter to Titus, he stresses the importance of three things for married women: turn to God, understand your role, and share within a community of women.

> As for you, promote the kind of living that reflects right teaching. . . . Teach the older women to live in a way that is appropriate for someone serving the Lord. They must not go around speaking evil of others and must not be heavy drinkers. Instead, they should teach others what is good. These older women must train the younger women to love their husbands and their children, to live wisely and be pure, to take care of their homes, to do good, and to be submissive to their husbands. Then they will not bring shame on the word of God. (Titus 2:1, 3–5)

If you follow this threefold plan, healing will break forth in your life, just as it did in mine. It doesn't matter whether your marriage is an oasis, a desert, or something in between. God faithfully uses a community of women and these principles to heal, strengthen, and encourage you.

TURN TO GOD

Because every marriage is unique, what works in one marriage may not be effective in another. Generic answers aren't going to work—you need specific answers, tailored to your situation. Where can you find marriage help this specialized?

Ruth Bell Graham, late wife of evangelist Billy Graham, found the help she needed by turning to God. In the words of her daughter, Ruth "made Christ her home, her purpose, her center, her confidant, and her vision." Because she turned to God, "Her happiness and fulfillment did not depend on her circumstances."[1]

Your happiness and fulfillment as a wife are founded on whether or not you turn to God in all the circumstances you face. When you fail to obtain help from God, you're left with only your own efforts to grow your marriage relationship. It won't be enough, trust me.

As a Christian, I struggled for many years trying to "be" a good wife. By doing the right things and saying the right words, I believed I could achieve a great marriage. My attempts were frustrated, however, by ignorance and sin. Exhaustion and despair forced me to accept the fact that I was unable on my own to fashion the marriage I desired.

Patiently, God waits for you and me to turn to Him and lean into His ability to save and heal. He will not force Himself into any area of our lives in which He hasn't been invited. God waits for you to tire of attempting the impossible on your own. He waits for you to ask for His help.

During a time when my husband and I needed God's help, we were discussing with friends the importance of turning to God and trusting in His ability to help with the big and small details of our lives. "After all," I blurted, "God generally does a good job!" After a brief moment of silence the others burst out in laughter. "He *generally* does a good job?" someone exclaimed sarcastically.

Do you feel that God has let you down in some way? Have you been running your life and marriage under the power of your limited strength and wisdom, thinking you will do a better job without His help? How is that working for you?

When you choose to do marriage on your own, to journey independently, it's as if you carry heavy chains around your neck, chains of wrong thoughts or imperfect knowledge you've acquired along the way. These chains are too heavy for you and they hold you back from having the kind of marriage you want. No matter how hard you try, your attempts are frustrated and often filled with pain. The shame of failure makes it difficult to move forward.

Adam and Eve, our first ancestors, experienced this too. In Genesis 3, we read about how they took matters into their own hands— trying out a life of independence—and failed. Immediately, they suffered shame and blame. The first marriage experienced the same painful consequences of independence that we experience when we try to do marriage on our own.

Isn't it ironic that, from a worldly perspective, *independence* is synonymous with *freedom*? Yet, in God's perspective, our independence leads to bondage and pain. You were not created to live independently from Him. He never intended you to go it alone.

As Christian wives, we discover there's a better way than doing marriage on our own. Howard Thurman once said, "There can be no personal freedom where there is not an initial personal surrender."[2] When we depend on God, relinquish control, and seek His leadership, we experience freedom—freedom from worry, fear, guilt, pain, and shame. In fact, God accomplishes more through us than we could ask, think, hope, or imagine.

When facing difficult situations in your marriage, picture Jesus removing the heavy chains of independence from your neck and saying: "I will free you from the work of figuring things out on your own. Now, you're free to respond to the situation knowing I love you and am with you. Allow Me to work through you to accomplish beautiful things."

Turn toward the One who loves you. Allow His love to flow through you so that you are able to love your husband despite your different personalities, communication styles, interests, strengths, and weaknesses.

How do you turn to God and receive His wisdom and power for your marriage? The Holy Spirit unfolded the following plan during a particularly difficult time in my marriage and it works wonders. You can turn to God by taking these four steps: be still, worship, read the Bible, and pray.

Be Still

Is it common for you to think through all the details of the problems that affect your marriage? Me too! Before we can receive God's wisdom and power, we need to still our anxious thoughts. Your thoughts won't help you like God's thoughts can. No plan you or I devise will work better than a God-inspired plan. Psalm 46:10 (NIV) says, "Be still, and know that I am God!"

When you catch yourself thinking through a problem, take a few deep breaths. The physical act of breathing deeply interrupts the trajectory of your worried thoughts and gives you opportunity to choose to redirect them toward God. Be still and focus on God who holds the answer to any problem you face.

Worship

Did you know you were created to worship and praise God? As a Christian, it's your highest priority. God isn't seeking the worship, but rather the worshipper. He wants you to draw near to Him and enjoy your relationship with Him so much that you overflow with praise.

What is worship? It is thanking God for who He is and what He does. Thankfulness and worship lifts your spirit, blesses God, and allows God's peace to fill your heart. Often when I stop and worship God, a plan takes shape in my heart even before I open my Bible and pray.

The Bible tells us that God inhabits the praise of His people (Psalm 22:3). Your worship invites Him into your problems. Your praise forms a throne from which He reigns. He rules with power in this place. You will actually sense His presence when you choose to praise Him. There's nothing like the presence of God to overcome a dark mood and fill you with hope. A woman who discovers the power that accompanies praise will be strengthened to love her husband when loving him is difficult.

If you're not used to praising God on your own, start out by telling God how thankful you are for His salvation—for all He did for you on the cross. Thank Him specifically for His daily blessings that you enjoy. Thank Him for your husband.

Also, praise Him for who He is. Who is God? He is awesome yet approachable, merciful, compassionate, our defender, an ever present help in time of trouble, and so much more. Record God's attributes—and corresponding Bible verses—in your prayer journal where they'll be easy to find in difficult times. According to Ruth Bell Graham, "Even contemplating what little we do comprehend of God dissolves doubts, reinforces faith and restores joy."[3]

Philippians 4:6–7 says, "Do not be anxious about anything, but in everything, by prayer and petition, *with thanksgiving*, present your requests to God. And the peace of God, which transcends all understanding, will guard your hearts and your minds in Christ Jesus" (NIV, emphasis mine). When you're consumed with worry over a problem, worship and praise draw your focus away from your obstacles and toward Christ, who is able to do above and beyond anything you could imagine (Ephesians 3:20). Worry never changes anything. Prayer with thanksgiving does.

Read the Bible

Many people think of the Bible as little more than a history book with lots of dos and don'ts thrown in to keep them in line. During the early years of my marriage, I much preferred romance novels to the Bible. I read the Bible because I felt it was my Christian duty, but

I didn't always alter my actions to fit its message. When I lost hope in my ability to repair my marriage, I turned to God. I surrendered my will and determined to follow His ways.

It was then that I read 1 Peter 3:1–2, "In the same way, you wives must accept the authority of your husbands, even those who refuse to accept the Good News. Your godly lives will speak to them better than any words. They will be won over by watching your pure, godly behavior." How can a wife get her message across without words? By living a godly life.

God empowered me to follow the instructions in this verse. I stopped nagging and preaching to Tom. Newfound strength and dignity invaded my heart as a result of my obedience to God's Word. Tom noticed the changes in my demeanor and behavior and responded positively. This, in turn, encouraged me to continue on this path.

Reading the Bible gives you wisdom for your marriage. If you are not in the habit of reading it daily, begin by reading five minutes a day. Here are a few passages to get you started:

+ Psalm 34:3–7
+ Proverbs 3:5–8
+ Matthew 7:1–5
+ John 14:15
+ 2 Timothy 2:21–22

If you're a new Christian, start reading the book of John to discover more about who God is and what He promises to those who believe in Him. Proverbs is another good place to start reading. It provides sound bites of wisdom for everyday matters that we face as wives. You can find a detailed description of God-honoring love in 1 Corinthians 13.

Read the passage slowly and attentively several times. If there are unfamiliar words or ideas, ask a mentor or pastor for some trusted resources to help you understand what you're reading. Then make it personal. Focus on a word or phrase that speaks to you in a personal way. Pray that the Holy Spirit will make God's Word clear to you.

Reflect on the word or phrase and gently repeat it to yourself. Allow it to interact with your thoughts, your hopes, your memories, your desires. When a few verses really touch me, I'll reread them for an entire week before moving on.

Meditating on God's Word will transform your thinking. Transformed thinking produces new actions. Gradually, you'll begin to experience the power and good results that come from obeying God's Word.

Pray

Prayer is talking to God. He is your personal Counselor, waiting for you to come into His office through the door of prayer. Little conversations with God will reveal much needed wisdom for the situations we face as wives.

Jesus said, "That's why I urge you to pray for absolutely everything, ranging from small to large. Include everything as you embrace this God-life, and you'll get God's everything" (Mark 11:24 MSG). Bring to God everything that concerns your marriage, and He will teach you how to live.

Last year, Tom and I had an argument that left me hurt and confused. Through prayer, I asked God to reveal to us any hidden sin in either of our hearts that may have caused the disagreement. Soon after I prayed, Tom apologized and took full responsibility for the argument.

God wants you to pray about absolutely everything because He cares! If my heart becomes heavy about anything, I roll my burdens onto God's outstretched arms. I experience relief when I give Him my concerns in prayer.

Communication with God is a two-way street—it includes giving and taking. Through prayer, you give your concerns to God, but you don't leave empty-handed! God wants to give you the answers you seek. So it's important not only to talk to God but also to listen for His guidance.

Spend quiet moments listening for His voice. Though few ever hear an audible voice, many sense it deep in their spirit. If you're unaccustomed to sitting quietly, it may take some time before your mind settles down to listen. It will take practice. Give your concerns to God and wait.

For the first eleven years of my marriage, I brought a lot of concerns to God but rarely allowed Him to teach me. Had I listened, I would have heard His thoughts about me and my role as a wife. He wanted to do good works through me. Because I wasn't as teachable as I thought, I forfeited the wisdom I needed so badly.

Since then, I've learned to listen to God with a journal and pen in hand. During prayer, I form a question based upon my concern, and then wait. Sometimes a verse of Scripture, a thought, a picture, or an impression penetrates my conscious mind. Whatever it is, I write it down. Sometimes it makes sense to me immediately, and sometimes my understanding doesn't come until later. If He instructs me to do something, I try to obey right away.

At other times, the answers I'm seeking don't come how or when I expect them. If you've experienced this, it doesn't mean that God isn't working through your prayers or that your faith is weak. Often, God answers in ways you don't expect. His timing is rarely yours. That's because His plans for you are much broader than you can imagine (Jeremiah 29:11) and He is working everything together for ultimate good (Romans 8:28). In times like these, you have an opportunity to deepen your faith by trusting Him. Trust God in prayer, and you will get God's everything—His comfort, peace, and the joy of knowing He's in control!

As you journey through marriage, I recommend you keep a prayer journal. You can journal in any type of notebook, of course, but if you choose *The Beautiful Wife Prayer Journal* for this season of your marriage, you'll find specific prayers and writing prompts and suggested Scripture to correspond to each chapter in *The Beautiful Wife*. As you consider these topics in more depth, it will help you seek God's will in your marriage.

As you reflect on God's answers to specific prayers, your trust and faith will grow. Referring back to this journal throughout the life of your marriage, you'll be reminded of all you have learned and you can avoid the hurt and confusion that results from doing things your way.

Turn to God by stilling your thoughts, worshipping, reading the Bible, and praying. Doing so provides a solid foundation for you, as a wife, to stand upon.

UNDERSTAND YOUR ROLE

When you said, "I do," you committed to fulfill an important, influential role which holds great purpose and destiny. But, "I do . . . what?" Just what God-designed role did you commit to fulfill?

If you want to strengthen your marriage, understanding your role in the marriage is absolutely critical. The role of wife is designed to be a combination of four important roles: equal partner, friend, helper, and prayer warrior.

Equal Partner

"So the LORD God caused Adam to fall into a deep sleep. He took one of Adam's ribs and closed up the place from which he had taken it. Then the LORD God made a woman from the rib and brought her to Adam" (Genesis 2:21–22). How God made Eve from Adam clues us in to how He intended a marriage relationship to work. Woman wasn't created from the man's head to rule over the man, nor was she created from his foot to be his doormat. Woman was created from man's rib to stand beside him as an equal, co-ruling with him on the earth. "You stand as an equal with man at the apex of God's created order."[4]

Though we are equal, we are not the same. Adam needed something he didn't already possess or there would have been no need for Eve. It is these differences that are the source of many challenges.

"If two people agree on everything, one of them is unnecessary," said Ruth Bell Graham. Billy responded by saying, "The sooner we accept that as a fact of life, the better we will be able to adjust to each other and enjoy togetherness."[5]

Somewhere in my husband's upbringing, he came to believe that when a husband and wife disagreed over an issue, it was the woman's role to back down. A wife could voice concerns if she voiced them ever so carefully, so as not to challenge her husband's thinking. If I were to decide on a course of action he disagreed with, Tom would be displeased and label me "unsubmissive." A wrong teaching on submission has confused many a man's and woman's thoughts on how to handle differences and disagreements.

An equal partnership produces the environment in which submission can flourish. This kind of relationship is in evidence among the Godhead. Jesus Christ is equal to God, yet He relinquished His will and submitted to the Father's will when He died on the cross. You must see yourself as an equal before you can choose to submit from a heart of love. Equality confers dignity upon submission.

In Ephesians 5, the infamous chapter on submission in marriage, Paul writes that husbands and wives are to submit to one another. The husband is to love the wife as Christ loves the church and laid down His life for her. The wife is to submit to her husband as she does to Christ. Neither person can force submission—it is a decision each must make.

God calls the husband to lay down his life for his wife—to put her needs above his own. But what do you do if your husband doesn't love you in this way? Never wait for your husband to obey God before doing so yourself! For the sake of your marriage, you can start the ball rolling. As you learn new biblical principles about your role as a wife in the following chapters, embrace them (submit to God) and God will transform you. Your husband will be impacted by your new behavior.

"God created man in his own image, in the image of God he created him; male and female he created them" (Genesis 1:27 NIV). You and your husband were both created in the image of God and are joint heirs of every good thing He offers. You are an equal partner with your husband in marriage, and your role holds great influence.

Friend

"GOD formed . . . all the animals of the field and all the birds of the air. He brought them to the Man to see what he would name them. . . . The Man named the cattle, named the birds of the air, named the wild animals; but he didn't find a suitable companion" (Genesis 2:20 MSG). Though Adam was surrounded by animals, even Rover couldn't give him what he needed most—companionship. Adam could only experience true companionship with someone who also bore God's image.

In order to maintain and grow my friendships with other women, we spend time together, doing things we enjoy—meeting for coffee, shopping, walking together. In the same way, "men place surprising importance on having their wives as recreational companions. . . . Spending recreational time with his wife is second only to sex for the typical husband."[6] When I was a busy wife with young children, it was easy to lose sight of the fact that Tom needed my companionship in recreational activities. Today, I see the deep need a man has for his wife to share his interests.

Women whom I admire sow seeds of friendship into their marriage by participating in their husbands' favorite activities. Some women learn to fish, while others read in the boat while their husbands fish. Many learn to golf, hike, bike, or ride in convertibles—despite bad hat hair! Some sit on bleachers watching their husbands compete in baseball or hockey games. I remember one woman saying she simply sat beside her husband while he watched Monday night football—and he gushed gratefulness for her company.

In addition to joining your husband in his favorite activities, you can also strive to find a hobby or passion you both share. One couple I know discovered that they both love to go birding, and this hobby has greatly benefited their marriage. Recently Tom and I developed a passion for eating healthy, natural foods. We now enjoy experimenting with new recipes together, shopping at farmer's markets, and taste-testing uncommon snacks from our local health-food store. Chopping vegetables side by side in the kitchen has deepened our friendship!

Is there a hobby or an interest that both you and your husband enjoy? Make time for it, talk about it, and nurture this shared passion in order to grow as friends.

Your husband needs a friend who will listen. Most men don't disclose their deep thoughts to other men. You need to be that friend. As a friend to your husband, you have great influence.

Helper

God made wives to be companions who would help their husbands. "And the LORD God said, 'It is not good for the man to be alone. I will make a companion who will help him'" (Genesis 2:18). This help goes well beyond housekeeping and hygiene. Robert Lewis describes it well in *The New Eve*:

> [The help a man] needs most to succeed in life is one that is distinctly feminine. It is a help that receives, admires, nurtures, responds, supports, and loves. A man grows by this kind of help. He matures. He is strengthened to reach higher and do more than he ever could without it. The truth is, every man longs for this kind of help.[7]

Zig Ziglar, known as one of the most impactful motivational speakers of all time and a best-selling author, loves his wife Jean and affectionately calls her "The redhead." Zig says of Jean, "She helps me be better at what I do."[8] Jean's intelligence is put to good use helping her husband hone his abilities. One way a wife helps her husband is by giving support and encouragement like Jean has given Zig. A wife who encourages her husband and praises his accomplishments will help improve his self-esteem.

At times it will also be necessary for you to help your husband by challenging him. Two heads really are better than one. "Woe to him who is alone when he falls, for he has no one to help him up." (Ecclesiastes 4:10 NKJV). If you see your husband heading down the wrong path, challenge him with loving encouragement.

When my husband was discouraged by his business's lack of success, it would have been destructive for me to support and encourage him to continue in a direction unsuited to his strengths and talents.

Instead, I challenged him to pursue a business model more in line with his abilities and passion.

Many wives have used their influential position as a helper to get their own way. If you're using your influence to get something *you* want or meet a need *you* have at the expense of seeking God's best in any given situation—stop! The results will be disappointing at best. Any action born from a selfish motivation is destructive to the marriage relationship. It can be easy to miss the fact that self-interest or selfishness lies beneath the "help" you give your husband. Ask God to help you determine if wrong motives are undermining your role.

A wife does herself harm by competing for control. A good helper will cooperate rather than compete with her husband, and that cooperation will mutually benefit them. A wife who helps her husband with the good of the marriage in mind has great influence.

Prayer Warrior

Prayer "is a way to invite God's power into your husband's life for his greatest blessing, which is ultimately yours, too."[9] It's not about getting your way, but getting God's way in the life of your husband. These are the selfless prayers that please God.

Years ago, I began praying for my husband. I'll admit some of my prayers were rather self-seeking. I wanted Tom to do this or buy that for me. You can ask for whatever you like, but if it's not God's will, you're not going to get it.

God answers prayers that agree with His Word. When you're reading the Bible, look for truths you want to see unfold in the life of your husband. In your prayer journal, set aside a special section devoted to verses you specifically pray for your husband. Seeing God's purposes fulfilled in his life will benefit you both much more than getting that leather sofa or piece of jewelry you have been wanting.

Pray daily for your husband's needs. Pray that his strengths will be used to bring glory to God and that his weaknesses will be strengthened and healed. Ask God to send him godly friends who will encourage his spiritual growth. Pray for his emotional and physical safety. Thank God for leading and guiding him in his roles as husband, father, and co-worker. Ask your husband if he has any needs you can pray for and then check back to see how things are going. He will be grateful to know you care about what's going on in his life and are faithfully praying for him.

If you want greater influence in the life of your husband, pray for him! Prayer is more effective than nagging, pleading, or arguing, and it fulfills your role to do him good rather than harm (Proverbs 31). Though it's often ignored except as a last resort, prayer is what gets the business of change done. Over the years, I've experienced many answers to prayers I prayed for Tom. You will too.

I hope your understanding of your role as a wife is deepening. By acting as an equal partner, friend, helper, and prayer warrior for your husband, you will fulfill the vows you made when you said, "I do."

SHARE WITHIN A COMMUNITY OF WOMEN

As a newly married woman, I longed to talk to someone about my marriage struggles, but I was afraid others wouldn't relate. I mistakenly believed everyone else's marriage was perfect. My own pain blinded me to the fact that everyone struggles to one degree or another during the life of their marriage.

Over time, I encountered a few women with whom I was able to develop a relationship of trust. Exposing my pain to them was like opening the emotional floodgates of my heart. The pressure that had built up for many years was finally released.

Within this community of women, I was able to ask questions about how to apply biblical teaching to my particular situation. Though they didn't always have concrete answers, I was comforted just knowing they cared. My burden was lightened when they prayed for me. Today, I still rely on godly mentors as Tom and I still encounter struggles in our marriage.

Because of my experience, I am passionate about bringing women together to find love, purpose, and hope within a community of women. When women gather together for godly mentoring, wonderful things happen. Recently, I asked a young woman to describe how her mentoring relationship impacted her life. Here is her story:

> I went through a difficult time three years ago, and it left me broken, hurt, depressed, and unable to trust God or those around me. Mentoring was the positive force in my life that gently guided me back to Jesus. Time spent with my mentor overwhelmed me with love and reminded me of my worth and purpose. She accepted me as I was and didn't judge me. During each mentoring session, I experienced relief from the burdens I came with because I was able to talk them through. I left our sessions with a game plan, and she held me accountable to follow through. My mentor is one of my biggest cheerleaders! Most of all, I see Jesus in her. He speaks guidance, love, and laughter through her. When I leave, it always feels like we had lunch with Jesus.
>
> My mentor has been very real and vulnerable with me so I feel safe to share openly. She doesn't pretend to know all the answers or just make something up. She is a friend who cares. She'll stop and pray for God's guidance when she doesn't know how to respond. Sharing her past and present experiences, I learn that I'm not alone in my struggles. When I'm in need of correction, she gives it in love—usually I don't even realize it happened until I'm on my way home!
>
> My mentor gives hope that God has good things in store for me.

In order for a community of women to experience the best God has to offer, three things must be present: humility, transparency, and accountability.

Humility

A community of women will flourish if it keeps God at its center. This is not the time for water-cooler-husband-bashing! God in-

structs us to examine our own lives before we figure out how to fix
our husbands:

> Why worry about a speck in your friend's eye when you have a
> log in your own? How can you think of saying, "Let me help
> you get rid of that speck in your eye," when you can't see past
> the log in your own eye? Hypocrite! First get rid of the log in
> your own eye; then perhaps you will see well enough to deal
> with the speck in your friend's eye. (Matthew 7:3–5)

When meeting with a community of women, I need to keep
my sharing focused on my *own* struggles and weaknesses, and resist
recounting all the imperfections of my husband. Personal change is
the only way to change my marriage.

That's not to say you can't speak about your husband, but exercise self-control and respect when you do. Be as brief and vague as
possible. Even sharing details of good things could embarrass your
husband if someone were to mention it to him! In order to qualify *if*
or *how* you should share information about your husband, consider
the words of Proverbs:

> The godly think before speaking; the wicked spout evil words.
> (15:28)
>
> A truly wise person uses few words. (17:22)
>
> A gossip goes around revealing secrets, but those who are trust-
> worthy can keep a confidence. (11:13)

Save your frustrations about your husband for your prayer journal. Pour them all out to the Lord. He cares about each one and
will attend to each detail you entrust to Him. Keep the group time
focused on your own issues.

With an attitude of humility, you'll protect your husband
as well as direct your energies where they will make the greatest

impact—in your life. The changes you make will ultimately benefit your marriage.

Transparency

In this age of perfection, do you keep your struggles under wraps to avoid exposing a less-than-perfect marriage and risking rejection from your friends? Even after our marriage improved, it was still difficult for me to admit to other women when Tom and I struggled over an issue. It's not easy to admit weakness. But, until you admit you have a problem, you cannot be helped. When you expose your struggles to others, you are in a prime position for healing.

Your transparency unlocks transparency in others. If the women who mentored me hadn't been honest about their own struggles, it would have been difficult for me to share openly. Because others were transparent, I was able to make that leap.

If you desire to experience intimacy within a community of women, you must move past the fear of vulnerability. Being real is the key to developing close relationships with women. The degree to which you are vulnerable is the degree of intimacy you will achieve.

Accountability

If you're serious about improving your marriage, you will submit to accountability within a community of women. Jesus reminds us in the Bible that it's not enough to hear good teaching—we must do what we've learned (Matthew 7:24–27). Knowing others are holding you accountable will give you the extra nudge you need to make changes that impact your marriage.

Women who embrace the First Steps at the end of each chapter in this book will see the results in their lives and marriages. But when your resolve flags or enthusiasm wanes, you need the support of other women to keep you accountable. Beautiful Womanhood small groups are designed for accountability. Report back to the group when you next meet about how your First Steps are going. Cheer each other on to nurture positive behavior patterns and choke off negative ones.

In the loving safety of a Beautiful Womanhood small group, one woman tearfully admitted that she had never uttered words of appreciation for her husband. She explained that she'd grown up in a home where much was expected, but little or no appreciation was given in return. On her way home from the group meeting, she called her husband to thank him for a kindness he had performed the previous day for a member of her extended family. At the following meeting, she was happy to report back to the group that she was focused on appreciating her husband.

If you are reading this book without the benefit of a mentor or small group, you can still grow and make changes as a wife that will impact your marriage. Journaling in *The Beautiful Wife Prayer Journal* will give you the opportunity to be mentored by God as you listen and reflect on all He desires to say to you through His Word.

As you journey through the next eleven chapters of *The Beautiful Wife*, you will encounter topics that are relevant to each and every marriage. Approach each chapter by turning to God, understanding your role, and sharing within a community of women. When you do, you will be equipped to journey through all the hills and valleys of your marriage, and you will be blessed!

1. When you find yourself in a difficult marriage situation, what is your first response? Who do you turn to first?
2. Think of a situation in your marriage when you relied on your own understanding to solve a problem, rather than turning to God for help. What was the result? How did this impact you and your marriage?
3. Have you experienced a time when God has spoken to you through His Word? Record these and other verses that encourage you in your prayer journal.

4. Do you regularly pray for your husband? Why or why not?
5. Have you experienced a time when God has answered prayers for you, your husband, or your marriage?
6. What's one small step you could take to actively fulfill your role as a wife?

First Steps

1. Read the Bible every day—even if only one verse. (If you don't already have a favorite Bible that you use for daily reading, *The New Women's Devotional Bible* from Zondervan offers fresh perspective on God's Word through a year's worth of relevant, engaging devotions to encourage you.
2. Let your husband know you'll be praying for him every day. Ask him if he has any needs you can pray about. Record his requests in the prayer journal. Pray for your husband every day! Thank God for your husband.
3. Write your prayer requests in the prayer journal, and record when and how God answers them.
4. Memorize Psalm 119:35. Write a response in your prayer journal.

Special Note

If you have never accepted Jesus as your personal Lord and Savior, I invite you to make a decision that will change your life as well as your eternal destiny.

The Bible tells us, "For all have sinned; all fall short of God's glorious standard. Yet now God in his gracious kindness declares us not guilty. He has done this through Christ Jesus, who has freed us by taking away our sins" (Romans 3:23–24).

God loves you so much that He sent His only Son to die on a cross to pay for your sins. He took your place so you would no longer be separated from Him—that's how much He desires a relationship with you. To begin a relationship with Him, you must acknowledge your sinfulness, ask for forgiveness and receive His gift of love by inviting Him to be Lord of your life. You can do so by praying like this:

Dear Lord Jesus, I know that I am a sinner and need Your forgiveness. I believe You died for my sins and rose from the dead, and one day are coming to take me to live with You forever. Forgive me and wash me white as snow. I invite You to come into my life and transform me by Your love. Help me to trust You as I share this love with those You place in my life. In Jesus' name I pray, amen.

If you prayed this prayer or one like it, talk to your mentor about your decision. Ask your Christian friends to support you, and find a church where you can be nurtured in your new faith. I also encourage you to visit www.crazylovebook .com or www.billygraham.org for more resources to help you grow in your relationship with Jesus Christ. God bless you!

If you have questions about Jesus and are not yet ready to make this decision, I encourage you to talk with your mentor about your questions. Above all, I desire that you enjoy an intimate relationship with Jesus Christ. No longer will you journey alone. Jesus Christ is there to love, protect, heal, and guide you—no matter the circumstances.

CHAPTER TWO

Attending to Self-Care

*And let me live whole and holy, soul and body, so I
can always walk with my head held high.*
—PSALM 119:80 MSG

*When the oxygen masks come down, put your own
mask on before attempting to help those around you.*
—FLIGHT ATTENDANT

I have just come inside from participating in a bit of self-care at the
clothesline. "The clothesline?" you might ask. Yes, the clothesline.
I make time to pin my clothes to a line because this activity deposits
something into my often weary soul as I drink in the sun, watch the
clouds, feel the breeze on my face, and inhale the lavender scent of my
wet laundry. This simple task feeds my physical, emotional, and spiritual self. I come inside feeling refreshed and energized. Sure, I could
save time using the dryer, but that doesn't "give" me anything.

Are you empty and in need of a deposit? Because you fulfill multiple roles—spouse, mother, housekeeper, employee, caretaker, and
friend—the constant juggling of these demands tends to increase the
physical, emotional, and spiritual pressures you feel. Most women
need to learn better ways of dealing with the stresses of caring about
everybody and everything.

When you don't practice good self-care, you cannot be the
wife you desire to be. It is difficult to be patient, kind, or happy—

sometimes you can't even have fun! You can't graciously or creatively handle complex emotional situations like conflict or misunderstandings because you are more likely to snap or shut down when you are tired and worn out. Self-care gives you peace, joy, and a sense of well-being, which in turn yields great dividends in your marriage, blesses your husband, and equips you to handle relationship challenges.

When you care for yourself spiritually, emotionally, and physically, you enable yourself to be the woman and wife you desire to be by preparing your spirit, mind, and body for all the new and exciting challenges that will be discussed in subsequent chapters.

Think of these three areas as circles of care. The spiritual nature is at the core of a woman and—while most others will never be aware of its condition—affects the emotional and physical natures. The next layer, the emotional nature of a woman, is seen only by some but impacts the outer layer, the physical nature of a woman, which everyone sees. Poor spiritual, emotional, and physical self-care causes a negative ripple effect from the inside out that prevents a woman from experiencing greater fulfillment in her marriage.

SPIRITUAL SELF-CARE

It's easy to ignore spiritual self-care, because spiritual needs are harder for others to distinguish than physical and emotional ones. However, the fact remains: you have a spirit that must be cared for. If your spirit is hardened through ignoring God's Word, your efforts to control your negative emotions will be fruitless. If your spirit is soft through consistent prayer, receptive to God's molding, even your ability to get the rest your body needs will be improved as you allow Him to handle your worries.

Because you live in a fallen world, sin wears away at your spirit.

Too many days without spiritual self-care leads to frustration, helplessness, and hopelessness that eats away at you and your marriage. When busyness or sin crowds out prayer and other spiritual activities, God's voice is muted by the louder voices shouting for your attention, and you miss out on hearing Him speak to you with guidance and comfort and forgiveness.

You needn't live this way. Take care of your spiritual needs by spending time alone with God, attending church, and developing godly friendships.

Quiet Time

Fill your spirit with life-giving fuel every day: spend time with God. Look on this time less as a routine and more as a quiet moment to search for God. During your quiet time, focus on filling your heart rather than your head. Tell God you need Him to replenish all you've given out. "God blesses those who realize their need for him, for the Kingdom of Heaven is given to them" (Matthew 5:3).

King David knew the satisfaction and joy that comes from spending quiet time with God. He wrote, "Satisfy us in the morning with your unfailing love, so we may sing for joy to the end of our lives" (Psalm 90:14). I have found satisfaction and joy in spending quiet time with God each day. He comforts my heart when I give Him my burdens. He frees me from the weight of sins when I confess them, for He always forgives me. He guides me through unfamiliar territory. When I give thanks to Him, I receive joy.

Luke 10:38–42 tells the story of two women, Mary and Martha, who hosted Jesus and His disciples one day. Mary sat at Jesus' feet, listening to every word He spoke. Martha was worrying over the big dinner she was preparing for everybody. She came to Jesus and told Him it seemed unfair that her sister sat around while she did all the work.

Jesus responded by saying, "My dear Martha, you are so upset over all these details! There is really only one thing worth being concerned about. Mary has discovered it—and I won't take it away from her." His response indicates the importance of caring for your spirit by spending time with Him. Don't deprive yourself of the one thing worth being concerned about!

Attend Church

The importance of attending a Bible-believing church cannot be overstated and is biblical. Hebrews 10:25 exhorts us *not* to neglect meeting together in regular worship. At church, you learn more about God and His Word. Crucial to spiritual development and maturity, listening to biblical teaching deepens your faith and refreshes your spirit. So many times, my pastor has shared a message that ministers to a specific need in my life or answers a particular question I've had and I leave church encouraged and strengthened to follow God.

Church is not only an important place to learn from God and His Word, it is also a place to fellowship with other believers and motivate each other "to acts of love and good deeds" (Hebrews 10:24).

Develop Godly Friendships

Godly friendships are critical for spiritual self-care. Women need friends with whom they can share their struggles and receive sound, biblical advice.

Sharing struggles with an unbeliever can be dangerous if the advice given is contrary to God's Word. Divorce is a contagious disease. If you only hang out with friends who are divorcing, chances are it's an option you may be more likely to consider yourself. Protect yourself, your husband, and your marriage by also spending time with godly friends committed to following Christ in their marriages.

It's also important to choose friends who are spiritually stronger than you. If you're the strongest Christian you know, it's time to find some new friends. Once my pastor gave the following illustration which stuck with me: Picture yourself on a platform. Someone from below the platform tries to pull you down, and does so easily. It's not hard to do. Now picture yourself trying to pull the person below you up onto the platform. It's much more difficult! The message? If most of your friends are unbelievers, they will have a strong downward pull on you and your choices. Trying to pull them and their choices upward is far more difficult.

Church is a good place to meet Christian friends. Your Beautiful Womanhood small group is also a good place to establish godly friendships. (If you are not in a Beautiful Womanhood small group, there is information in the back of this book about how to join one.)

Care for yourself spiritually through spending quiet time with God, attending church, and developing godly friendships. Doing so gives you the wisdom, strength, and encouragment you'll need to effectively fortify your emotions and physical body.

EMOTIONAL SELF-CARE

The year 2006 ushered unwelcome emotions into my life. My husband was unhappy in his job, two of my grown children were making poor choices, my mother-in-law was showing signs of Alzheimer's, extended-family issues were surfacing, and I was writing a book. As the year exploded, our marriage suffered. Self-care became vital for my emotional preservation and the protection of our marriage.

What weighty emotions are you carrying: fear, guilt, shame, envy, anger, sadness? The Bible tells us, "A calm and undisturbed mind and heart are the life and health of the body, but envy, jealousy, and wrath are like rottenness of the bones" (Proverbs 14:30 AMP). What should you do when your emotions go wild and threaten your stability?

Uncover the Source

When we experience sadness, anger, guilt, shame, envy, or fear, it's important to acknowledge the source of our feelings and move toward our pain. Our natural inclination is to escape or medicate, but our emotions don't fizzle out simply because we changed our location or buried them with our drug of choice (food, alcohol, movies, books, activities, shopping, etc.). They will resurface to scream another day.

While two of my adult children were making poor choices, I came face-to-face with guilt and shame. I'd had high hopes for their future with God, but now, weighed down by their disappointing actions, I cowered in guilt and shame. I wanted to hide.

My pain motivated me to talk to a Christian counselor who encouraged me to face my emotions (you'll need encouragement—this isn't easy). She helped me discover that I learned as a child to cover up sin, rather than risk rejection from exposed failures. As a mother, I repeated this childhood pattern. When my kids participated in sinful behavior, I'd control the damage by hiding it so as not to risk others' rejection. When I lacked the control to cover my adult children's sin, I wanted to hide in shame. Move over, Adam and Eve!

God will work through your emotions if you let Him. If you stop running from them and face them head on, He will be there to comfort, help, and heal you through the process. If I discover that my own sin is the root of my emotions, I confess it and He forgives me. If the emotions are from some other root, I let them go.

It's been a positive experience to uncover and deal with the source of my weighty emotions. I've grown stronger. I'm cleansed from sin, enjoying increased freedom and finding acceptance among the women I talk to.

Uncover the source of your emotions, move toward your pain, and allow God to heal and free you.

Rein in Your Thoughts

In the difficult circumstances of life, Satan tempts you with all kinds of fear. It's his most effective weapon against you. If the devil can steal your peace of mind, he's got your joy, and a joyless woman is a defeated woman.

In my situation with my adult children, I feared others' rejection and judgment, and so I lost my peace and joy. I dodged women I knew at church. I was tempted to lay down my ministry, and I was unhappy at home.

Your thought life is your own—take charge of it! The Bible talks about the importance of paying attention to your thoughts. If you're not careful about what you're thinking, your thoughts can lead you into trouble (wrong actions). It's important to think about what you're thinking before you act!

Philippians 4:8 tells us to concentrate on things that are "true and honorable and right" and to "think about things that are pure and lovely and admirable" and "that are excellent and worthy of praise." When you replace your thoughts with God's thoughts, your actions will reflect God and His ways. A series of godly actions will eventually lead you out of distress.

When I'm tempted to fear, I remind myself that God says "Do not fear" or "fear not" 365 times throughout the Bible. He means it and you can believe it! Meditating on these words settles my mind and soothes my emotions: *There is nothing to fear. Fear not. Don't be afraid . . .*

I also remind myself that God isn't surprised at the situations that have surprised me. He knows all my days—even the bad ones. And He promises to turn all things—even the bad things—into good for those who love Him (Romans 8:28). God is not shocked or dismayed. He's not at a loss for what to do next. That knowledge calms me, and I can begin to act like a trusting daughter again.

Rein in your thoughts and think God's thoughts before you act. It will calm your troubled mind and produce positive actions.

Tame Your Tongue

You exercise power over your emotions with what you say, for good or harm. Joyce Meyer says, "Every time you open your mouth, you are ministering death or life, and whatever you dish out is what you are going to eat."[1]

When I said to myself, "I'm embarrassed to run into people I know at church," my words produced the *action* of embarrassment. When I began to say, "I'm more than a conqueror through Christ

Jesus who loved and saved me," I *acted* like a conqueror. A simple change of vocabulary helped me straighten up, look people in the eyes, and stretch out my hand to take theirs. In taking their hand, I often learned of their struggles and was able to encourage them with my own story. As a result, I experienced an increased sense of well-being as I interacted with others who could relate to me.

Take inventory of your words and make sure they convey the thoughts and words found in the Bible. God's words silence unruly emotions and change our actions.

Get the Help You Need

We've all been through—or are currently going through—difficult times that stress the mind and emotions. If you're having difficulty moving *through* your valley of the shadow of darkness (Psalm 23:4), you may need help and encouragement to see the light as I did.

Don't accept being overwhelmed. Find those who can help meet your needs for emotional self-care. Many churches have pastoral counselors or can recommend Christian counselors that offer sound, biblical guidance for the struggles you face.

Exercise good emotional self-care: uncover the source of negative emotions, rein in your thoughts, tame your tongue, and get the help you need. You will be strengthened with an increased sense of well-being.

PHYSICAL SELF-CARE

It's human nature to take good health for granted until you're affected by sickness. I was reminded of this recently when I was afflicted with bronchitis. Once diagnosed, I realized I'd sacrificed my physical well-being to meet a deadline.

Physical self-care means taking care of your body through a healthy diet, exercise, and rest. Negligence in these areas often leads to sickness and premature aging, which will hinder or prevent you from accomplishing all you hope to.

Healthy Diet

What do you eat? Are you a self-proclaimed junk-food junkie? There is good reason to take your diet seriously. When you don't eat well, your body slowly deteriorates—it ages faster. Aging faster prevents you from keeping up with all the demands you face.

When we're young, we don't often worry about what we put into our bodies. As we age, however, we discover the doctor's report card on our physical health is no longer straight A's. If you want to live a long, strong, healthy life, pay attention to your diet now! "A prudent person foresees the danger ahead and takes precautions; the simpleton goes blindly on and suffers the consequences" (Proverbs 22:3).

There are great resources available at your library or bookstore on the subject of diet and nutrition. I'll simply highlight a few foundational principles here.

What is God's idea of a healthy diet? In Genesis, God says to Adam and Eve, "Look! I have given you the seed-bearing plants throughout the earth and all the fruit trees for your food" (1:29). He's talking fruits and veggies. Have you heard about Daniel from the Bible? He ate a steady diet of fruits and vegetables and was healthier than the men who ate the king's choice foods. I'm not implying that you must become a vegan, but you can't go wrong by increasing your intake of food from plants.

Beyond increasing your intake of fruits and vegetables, another good principle is that it's best to eat foods in their most natural state. Choose whole grains rather than processed, potatoes rather than potato chips, and strawberries and bananas rather than prepackaged fruit snacks. This isn't law but rather a guide to healthier choices.

A decision to make healthier food choices requires planning. Plan your shopping lists—don't wait until you get to the store to decide what to buy. If I wait until I'm in the grocery store to plan my meals, I gravitate to preassembled meals, which are significantly less healthy.

If you find yourself at the grocery store without a plan, you can avoid unhealthy choices by focusing the majority of your shopping on the perimeter of the store. This is generally where the healthy foods are located, away from the cans and boxes of the center aisles.

If you're like me, you may need inspiration when it comes to meal planning. The programs featured on the Food Network television station inspire me to plan for the week's meals. I also refer to cooking magazines and cookbooks I've collected over the years. The Internet is awash with websites devoted to recipes and meal planning such as epicurious .com, and if you google a list of ingredients you have on hand, you'll be directed to an entire list of websites where you'll find ideas for combining them. I just tried this myself by typing in "cauliflower, celery, and chicken stock." In a matter of seconds, a list of related sites popped up. After clicking on one, I discovered a tempting cauliflower soup recipe (don't balk unless you've tried it!). On the same site, I learned I can prepare my own brining solution for my Thanksgiving turkey—which I usually pay a small fortune for at Williams-Sonoma!

If you're not accustomed to thinking about what you buy and put into your body, take baby steps.

+ Reduce your intake of junk food.
+ Avoid foods with high sugar content.
+ Replace margarine and butter with olive oil.
+ Eliminate one "bad food" from your diet each year—a few years ago Tom and I stopped drinking pop. The following year we cut back on fatty meat.

If your diet doesn't fuel your body to meet all the challenges of being a wife, begin taking small steps to improve the way you eat. What baby step can you take to make healthier food choices?

Exercise

When I get busy, I often cross exercise off my to-do list before I've even begun my day. I'm tempted to believe it doesn't benefit anyone but me, and it's not all that fun. Unless you're high on exercise, you'll need motivation to keep it a priority.

Where can you find this motivation? Christian wellness professional Ruth McGinnis says, "Nobody can motivate another person. You have to have that inner desire for a healthier life. But one motivation that works for almost everyone is fear—the fear of losing your range of motion, the fear of high cholesterol or high blood pressure."[2]

A sedentary lifestyle is to blame for many of the health problems experienced by women:

+ *Muscle loss.* Muscles atrophy with lack of use, and since muscle burns fat, you'll pack on more pounds if you don't move your body.
+ *Bone loss.* You can build bone mass until you're 35—and help maintain or slow the loss of your bone density in the years after—with weight-bearing exercises. Want a hip, spine, or wrist fracture in your senior years? No? Get out those dumbbells! I have.
+ *Depression.* Exercise increases the serotonin levels in your brain. With more serotonin, you feel more optimistic. An optimistic woman is a happier wife.

As I age, I realize the importance of maintaining my body through exercise. Though my body doesn't look like it once did (and that's okay), I don't want to gain weight, lose muscle mass, or feel tired all the time. I want to fully participate in life with my husband. This motivates me to exercise.

If you're going to incorporate exercise into your demanding schedule, you'll have to find a plan that works for you. I don't like traveling to a gym, so I exercise at home. I get bored easily, so I rotate between walking, biking, and following a televised exercise program. When my kids were small, I'd watch an exercise video first thing in the morning while they were playing. Sometimes I'd walk around the block while I pulled them in a wagon.

There are lots of ways to build more activity into your daily life:

+ During winter months, walk the halls of your local mall before the shops open.
+ Exercise with a girlfriend—it'll make exercising enjoyable and keep you more accountable.
+ When parking, choose a spot farther from your destination.
+ Take the stairs instead of the escalator or elevator.
+ If you work outside the home, take your walking shoes and see if a co-worker would like to walk with you during lunch.
+ Join a gym.
+ Buy a Leslie Sansone walking video[3] and walk indoors. A friend of mine lost over sixty pounds that way!
+ Walk or bike with your husband after dinner.

Investing in exercise is not a luxury—it is an absolute necessity! Move your body and experience the multiple benefits of strength, vitality, and optimism.

REST

Do you fill every waking minute with activity, or do you carve out time for rest? Because God cares about our rest, He instituted a weekly Sabbath day of rest—a gift for His people. Jesus said, "The Sabbath was made to benefit people" (Mark 2:27); and, "Come to me, all of you who are weary and carry heavy burdens, and I will give you rest" (Matthew 11:28). Do you accept God's gift of rest in your life?

Downsize Your Schedule

Even if you enjoy everything on your agenda, if it is too full you are stressing your body. An overwhelming schedule keeps your body's stress response—increased adrenaline and heart rate to help you meet challenges—constantly turned on. Don Colbert, MD, said, "When your stress response gets stuck, you may experience fatigue and/or insomnia, depression, obesity, heart disease (the number one killer of women), high blood pressure, or irritable bowel."[4] Avoid these terrible effects of stress and use wisdom when scheduling your life!

What areas of your busy life cause you stress?

+ Track where your time goes by jotting down what you're doing every half hour for several days. Look for time-devouring sinkholes like reading blogs or watching television. Ask yourself, "Is this the best way to be spending my time?"
+ Identify what you like to do. Make a list of activities you've participated in over recent months. Determine which ones energize and excite you and which ones drain you.

Your schedule and stress are affecting your interactions (or lack thereof) with your husband. When talking with young wives, I'm overwhelmed by their oftentimes self-imposed busyness. Marriage, like any relationship, cannot grow and strengthen if it is not given time.

Pray and evaluate where you could cut back on your commitments. Your children will live (without regret) if they participate in only one extracurricular activity or none at all. Care for yourself by controlling your stress level—it will benefit you and your relationship with your husband.

Sleep

The best advice is old advice: you'll function well on *eight hours* of sleep per night. When you function better you enjoy life more. Professor of psychology Norbert Schwarz, PhD, discovered through a University of Michigan study that "making sixty thousand more in annual income has less of an effect on your daily happiness than getting one extra hour of sleep a night."[5] If sleep makes you happier, why aren't you hitting the hay earlier?

For many, technology is to blame. Television and the Internet keep women up late at night. I get many emails from young women after 11:00 p.m. Because women are largely others-focused, you wait until the "others" are in bed before you'll care for yourself.

Change your daily routine so you can change your evening routine and start keeping a regular bedtime that is better for you.

- Exercise during the day—it helps you sleep better.
- Turn off the laptop or TV an hour earlier.
- Drink a cup of decaffeinated herbal tea.
- Take a warm bath.
- Give your husband a massage and request the same.
- Make to-do lists before bed so the details of tomorrow don't keep you awake.

Get enough sleep. It is good for you and helps you cope better with life and marriage.

You Time

Who has time for downtime? You should—after you downsize your stressful schedule. Personal time isn't a luxury—it's a necessity. Just a few moments of peace and quiet every day can make you more patient and able to deal with the demands of life.

"You time" is time spent doing something that nurtures you and gives you pleasure. Listen to music that stirs your soul. Dance to a great song. Hang your clothes on a line.

"You time" doesn't have to come in large quantities. It can be the difference between a ten-minute shower and a twenty-minute bath. Keep in mind that no one can give you *"you time"* except you.

When you improve your diet, exercise more, and take time to rest, your joy increases and your sense of well-being improves. These will greatly enhance your relationship with your husband—and with others.

Overall, the practice of good, consistent spiritual, emotional, and physical self-care is the best thing you can do for yourself and your marriage.

It's time for me to head out to the clothesline again!

1. What evidence have you seen in your life that your spiritual condition affects your emotional and physical conditions?

2. What do you need to do to ensure regular spiritual self-care? Write it down.

3. Are you experiencing any of the following emotions: guilt, shame, envy, anger, sadness, or fear? If so . . .

   - What is your response: Escape (books, television, Internet, busyness)? Medication (shopping, activity, eating, drinking alcohol)?
   - Can you remember the source of this emotion? If so, record it in your journal. If not, ask God to reveal it.
   - When you're feeling this emotion, what do you tell yourself? Write your response. Does it line up with God's Word? If not, what does God's Word say to correct your response?

4. What small steps are you willing to take to improve your diet?

5. What motivates you to exercise? Which steps could you take to follow through?

6. How is your stressful schedule impacting your marriage? What one activity could you eliminate? Journal a response.

7. What prevents you from getting eight hours of sleep? How does a lack of sleep affect your marriage? What small step could you take to increase the hours you sleep?

8. Which *"you time"* activity gives you pleasure and refreshes you? How often do you participate in this activity? What could you do to make it a regular part of each day? Respond in your prayer journal.

First Steps

1. Spend quiet time with God each day. Throughout the rest of the day, think on one thought His Word inspires.

2. Uncover the source of unhealthy emotions. Journal your discoveries. If you need help uncovering the source of emotional pain, discuss with your husband your need to see a Christian counselor or pastor.

3. Do something active three times a week. If you can't exercise during the day, ask your husband to watch the kids at night so you can walk or bike for twenty to thirty minutes to improve your physical fitness, strength, and overall health.

4. Eliminate one bad food from your diet. Share with your husband your ideas for healthier eating.

CHAPTER THREE

Living as the Genuine Article

So, chosen by God for this new life of love, dress in the
wardrobe God picked out for you: compassion, kindness,
humility, quiet strength, discipline. Be even-tempered,
content with second place, quick to forgive an offense.
Forgive as quickly and completely as the Master forgave you.
And regardless of what else you put on, wear love. It's your
basic, all-purpose garment. Never be without it.
—Colossians 3:12 MSG

Esse quam videri.
To be, rather than to appear.
—Plato, *The Republic*

Years ago, I received a Christmas newsletter written by Lisa Whelchel, the former child star of *The Facts of Life*. I remember it still. Why? Because in it Lisa demonstrated something I rarely see: genuineness. She removed her mask in order to reveal the real Lisa—the genuine article— the Lisa who struggles with overspending, overeating, and tough family situations. Because of that, I identified with her and heard the message of truth she expressed. Not once was I tempted to reject her because her life's pieces didn't add up to perfection. Instead, I respected her willing-ness to share her struggles for the benefit of others.

Most women are not that free in revealing themselves to their husbands and close friends, much less the general public. It feels much safer to hide behind a mask. Unfortunately, in this arena, what feels safe is actually dangerous. Hiding sin, rather than exposing it to God's light and the safety of His love, prevents necessary healing from taking place. Unattended, sin can grow and spread, infecting other areas of your life. John and Stasi Eldredge, authors of *Captivating: Unveiling the Mystery of a Woman's Soul*, point out that we lose intimacy not only with others but also with God when we hide behind the mask of what we think others expect of us or behind the image of who we want others to think we are.[1] The creator of the universe has no desire to have intimacy with my mask but with my real self.

LIFE BEHIND A MASK

Do you hide behind a mask? It's a regular way of life for many women. We're drawn to masks when we let fears alarm us, particularly the fear that we'll be rejected because of our flaws. The problem is, when we assume a false identity to gain acceptance, we lose honest relationships. Once started, the work to keep up the masquerade is never-ending and, frankly, exhausting. Joy and freedom are sacrificed on the altar of acceptability.

You may successfully deceive others, but you can't fool God. He knows who you really are. He longs to tenderly remove the mask you wear, reveal the authentic you, and heal the wounds you've been hiding. The "woman behind the mask"—the one who struggles with fear, addiction, unforgiveness, anger, selfishness, envy, and the like—is the woman with whom Jesus desires to have a relationship. He accepts you just as you are. He wants you to experience His love, and He wants to help you grow to trust Him with your life.

What mask do you hide behind?

Superwoman

Do you wear the mask of Superwoman—going above and beyond the call of duty so others will be pleased and happy with you?

Often, the motive for this behavior is to gain praise in an attempt to increase our feelings of self-worth. Underneath this mask is a frightened, hurting woman who believes that she wouldn't be accepted as she really is.

If you give your public image "superpowers" in an attempt to bolster people's affections for the real you behind the mask, you are doomed to failure. You'll find that you despise the real you more than ever for not being able to live up to the Superwoman image everyone admires. As one young woman wrote me, "I wish I were Superwoman and could handle everything with grace and peace. But, I'm not. So I find myself stressed and overwhelmed."

Many women who wear the Superwoman mask forsake the needs of their husbands in order to busily serve others. These overcommitted Superwomen often find themselves exhausted. What kind of intimacy will you have with your husband or with others if you are stressed and overwhelmed? You'll be too busy and exhausted to enjoy the important relationships in your life—the very things that will give you the sense of self-worth you are seeking.

The Superwoman mask also blocks an intimate relationship with our Heavenly Father. You will never experience intimacy with God if you can't approach Him except under the cover of your works. Remember that since "[you] are saved by God's kindness, then it is not by [your] good works. For in that case, God's wonderful kindness would not be what it really is—free and undeserved" (Romans 11:6).

What are you busy with? Does all of your work bring you joy and fulfillment? If you're involved with things which God has not chosen specifically for you, it raises the question, What has God chosen you to do that's not getting done? Maintaining a role that you haven't been assigned places you at odds with God's plan for your life. It's not a good fit. Until you're living out God's plans for you, you will not experience the fullness of peace and joy in your work.

Is wearing the Superwoman mask working for you? Do you feel closer to God or to your husband because of your many works? Allow God to remove your mask and minister to your tired soul.

Material Girl

Are you a Material Girl living in a material world? Most American women are, to one degree or another. We spend money to buy things we don't need in an effort to impress people—many of whom we don't even like! American culture is saturated with consumerism; this makes the Material Girl mask difficult to shed. It's hard to gain a healthy perspective in a land where billions of advertising dollars are spent to capture your attention and convince you that your kitchen, clothing, and car are now outdated.

How much have you bought into the culture's message? Do you wear the Material Girl mask in an attempt to appear more acceptable or more successful to others?

There was a time when I wouldn't invite people over for dinner because my house wasn't all that I wanted it to be. If I thought their home was newer, bigger, or better decorated than mine, they might not get an invitation. It was self-protection. I didn't want to give someone the chance to decide I didn't measure up because my house didn't fit in *House Beautiful* or *Better Homes and Gardens*.

The Material Girl mask can put a strain on your relationship with your husband. Unless you have an unlimited budget, your desire to have what you want when you want it adds stress to his life.

This mask can also keep you from experiencing intimacy with others. If you base your value on the designer labels you wear—or the expensive items you own—you've crafted a superficial environment in which to develop friendships. You'll always fear someone might have something better than you, and fear definitely has a negative impact on intimacy.

Materialism affects our intimacy with God, too. He's given us everything we have, and He calls us to use it wisely. When we use the money He's entrusted to us to gild our self-image rather than using it for the purpose He gave it to us, these gifts come between us and God. We forget that "God prospers [us] not to raise [our] standard of living, but to raise [our] standard of giving."[2]

Jesus explained why the way we spend our money impacts our

intimacy with God. "Don't store up treasures here on earth, where they can be eaten by moths and get rusty, and where thieves break in and steal. Store your treasures in heaven, where they will never become moth-eaten or rusty and where they will be safe from thieves. Wherever your treasure is, there your heart and thoughts will also be" (Matthew 6:19–21). When our treasure lies where God's heart is, our heart and thoughts will be unified with His—the picture of intimacy.

When we remove the Material Girl mask and begin using the resources God's entrusted to us for His purposes, we experience joy and freedom. "Paul says that being 'generous' and 'willing to serve' and 'rich in good deeds' allows us to 'take hold of the life that is truly life.' As opposed to what? The second-class, so called 'life' of materialism. . . . Giving is the only antidote to materialism."[3]

Removing this mask requires you to recognize that your value is not determined by the brand of your clothes or the value of your possessions. God sees you as His unique and amazing creation who was worth dying for. Peel away the Material Girl mask; it will bring you closer to God, your husband, and others.

The Perfect Ten

The mask I was most tempted (and am sometimes still tempted) to wear is the Perfect Ten mask—the mask which gives the impression that I've got it all together. I'm great. Everything about my life is great: my marriage, my children, my home-life, my work, my relationship with God. I've got life by the tail; I'm totally in control and blessed by God.

When I wore this mask, I was more concerned with *appearing* perfect than with making way for Christ's redemptive work in my life. The mask wasn't just about convincing others; it was also about convincing myself that I was okay. It kept me insulated from the coldness and desperation of my true condition. I was lying to myself. I exerted Herculean effort to generate this illusion. Mustering up perfection is futile for humans with a sinful nature. It was all so discouraging.

If it was so ineffective, what drove me to keep this mask in place?

A huge dose of fear and pride. I was afraid others would reject me if they saw my imperfections, and I proudly wanted to be independent rather than recklessly abandoned to God.

My fear was understandable, considering humankind's propensity to love conditionally. It can be difficult to imagine that anyone, let alone Jesus, desires relationship with us, flaws and all—but it's true. Do you know the story of Jesus and the Samaritan woman at the well (John 4:7–42)? She said she was unmarried—she masked the fact that she'd been married five times and was currently living with a man who was not her husband. Jesus gently exposed the truth, not to condemn her, but to build a real relationship with her. He continued to talk with her and her friends for two days. Just as Jesus desired a relationship with the Samaritan woman, He longs for an honest relationship with the unvarnished you.

What about my pride, which fueled my independence? Though I longed to "do it myself," my attempts to live perfectly were futile and produced brokenness and despair. Nothing I did could make or keep me white as snow. It was the same for the Samaritan woman, and it's the same for you. Our only hope is Jesus, who asks us to humble ourselves and depend on Him to *make* us clean, rather than using masks to *appear* clean. When we do, we experience joy and peace, for He heals all the wounds hidden by our masks.

We don't always want to involve ourselves with imperfect people or messy relationships. It reminds us of our own vulnerabilities and sin-ravaged natures. Unfortunately, when we ignore or withdraw from hurting people, it only reinforces their belief that a Perfect Ten mask is indispensable—further keeping them from an authentic relationship with Christ and others.

There are no perfect people in this world, but there are many who dishonestly portray themselves as having it all together. As Christians, we need to be the first to shed our masks and openly share our wounds and weaknesses. Being authentic will open us up to Christ's healing and strength, and will invite others to share openly with us as well.

WHO, ME?

Maybe you're like me, and you don't always realize when you're wearing a mask. God has used difficulties in my life to show me a mask I'm wearing and to remind me that I won't experience a fulfilled life behind it. During a particularly difficult time, He showed me I was wearing a mask to cleverly conceal my issues.

At the time, my life was full of turmoil. My daughter was going through a painful experience that affected me deeply, yet one which I could not fix or control. When I spent time with God, I did most of the talking. Nonstop panic prayers formed most of my communication with Him. Because of His great love for me, He didn't force me to be quiet and listen. He waited for me to tire of doing things in my own strength.

When I sought help and guidance, I learned about Listening Prayer in Mary Geegh's book, *God Guides*. Through Listening Prayer, I began to understand that God wanted my companionship. He wanted a closer relationship with me. He longed for me to wait in His presence and listen to Him.

Once I began listening to God and He had my full attention, I was amazed at what He said. He spoke to me about the Perfect Ten mask I was wearing and the issues I was hiding behind it—much like He addressed the issues in the life of the Samaritan woman. What He revealed to me caught me by surprise! I lacked compassion, humility, and the willingness to forgive.

I was a seasoned Christian; you would think compassion, humility, and a willingness to forgive wouldn't be new territory for me. Though I'd exercised these character traits to a point, I still had a long way to go in practicing them in all areas and when the pressures of life increased. I was able to appear like I had it all together; why couldn't other women do the same? I'd focused so much energy on generating that perfect image, I'd been oblivious to cancerous cells of pride growing rampantly behind my mask.

Once I recovered from the shock of exposure, I discovered that I didn't feel condemned by God. I felt overwhelmed by His love. This resulted in a full-blown conviction to change and remove the Perfect Ten mask. I experienced His great love for me in the midst of my weakness and failure, and this knowledge spurred me forward.

> For now I [God] just want you to be with me and discover that our relationship is not about performance or you having to please me. I'm not a bully, not some self-centered demanding little deity insisting on my own way. I am good, and I desire only what is best for you. You cannot find that through guilt or condemnation or coercion, only through a relationship of love. And I do love you.[4]

Even though I never experienced condemnation from God about the real me under the mask, I wasn't sure I'd be as well received by people. As I grew in the experiential knowledge of His love, I began to realize it didn't matter what others thought of me as long as He loved me. Still, actually moving past the fear of living without a mask was one of the greatest challenges of my life. God knew I needed help with this one. And so, through a series of seemingly unrelated circumstances, He took me on a journey where I discovered the joy and power of living as the Genuine Article.

MY JOURNEY OF REMOVING THE MASK

Early in 2007, I was asked to lead a women's conference in Uganda. My husband wasn't sure if traveling to Africa was a good idea, so we committed it to prayer. While we were listening for an answer, I sensed God asking me to fast from spending, except for groceries, for thirty days. Sometimes you know that you've heard God's voice because you'd never have come up with those words on your own. This was one of those times. I'd never heard of a fast from spending. Tom needed no convincing that a fast from spending came directly from the mouth of God. He still gets excited just thinking about it!

During the fast, it became clear I had used spending as a way to gain a comfort fix. When I was spending money, I felt carefree and lighthearted. Instead of dwelling on the unpleasantness in my life, I was thinking of my purchases and how they would bring me pleasure. Not until I stopped spending did I realize how short-lived the fix really was. During the fast, when I felt the urge to spend—to anesthetize my pain—I pictured myself running into the arms of Jesus, the Great Comforter. Oh, what comfort I received!

One night, I told good friends my experience of gaining comfort through the power of the Holy Spirit rather than money. I exclaimed that I had never felt so comforted. One friend then told us about a dream he'd had shortly after hearing about the invitation from Uganda. After the dream, he had awoken and recorded the following thoughts:

". . . this is for Sandy. Christ's redemption of women is beautiful. Beautiful Womanhood is a result of redemptive wholeness. The visuals the ministry uses on the books, etc., are like a piece of beautifully veneered furniture. There is something going on with the ministry to the brokenness of abused women. In Uganda, there are hurting, abused women, and something is connecting their need and Beautiful Womanhood. Though there is nothing wrong with veneer, it is only the topping—the covering, and without good structure it is shallow and will not hold up. It is time to add a new depth to the ministry."

Then these verses came to my friend's mind:

All praise to the God and Father of our Lord Jesus Christ. He is the source of every mercy and the God who comforts us. He comforts us in all our troubles so that we can comfort others. When others are troubled, we will be able to give them the same comfort God has given us. You can be sure that the more we suffer for Christ, the more God will shower us with his comfort through Christ. (2 Corinthians 1:3–5)

When my friend was finished sharing, everyone in the room broke down in tears, praising God for His work in my life. I'd learned to listen and God had spoken. I'd obeyed, and He'd acted. When He acted, I was changed. He had replaced my illusion of perfection with the reality of His redemptive work, and it was upon this foundation that He would build the Beautiful Womanhood ministry—a ministry He wanted to use in the lives of women in Africa.

I packed my bags.

For the conference theme, the Ugandan church had chosen, "The Impact of Women in Ministry." While prayerfully preparing for my session, I sensed God asking me to break the subject down into three parts: women, ministry, and impact. Based on Matthew 13, I spoke about how a woman must deal with the rocks and thorns in the soil of her heart, or her ministry will be adversely affected, diminishing the impact which otherwise might have been.

I openly shared with the women in Uganda that the Lord had recently revealed to me rocks and thorns in the soil of my heart. The rock of offense was buried deep in my heart. If someone hurt me, I would be offended and hold their action against them, sometimes for many years. I got along fine until problems or persecution came my way, and then I'd be offended at the one who caused me trouble or pain. Buried offenses blocked God's marvelous love from rooting deep in my heart.

I also exposed to them the thorns that threatened to choke all fruitfulness in my life: the false comfort of spending money that I had discovered during my spending fast. In anguish over my daughter's struggles, in need of comfort, I'd turned not to my Comforter but to wealth.

As I shared my failings and weaknesses with a vulnerable spirit, the women's eyes were riveted on me. They hung on every word I spoke. The women of Uganda could relate to my struggle of hanging onto offenses. Many of them had suffered far worse offenses than I had ever had to deal with. Through my candid sharing, God touched them, and they were convicted to forgive their offenders.

One woman said she'd believed God loved white people more than black people because white people didn't face the struggles that black people did. Because of my testimony, she began to understand that trouble is not limited by the color of one's skin. The light of God's love had dawned on her life. Another woman revealed that in the past God had called her to minister to other women. However, because her own children weren't leading exemplary lives, she felt disqualified. That day at the conference, she recommitted her life to the ministry God had given her.

This experience revealed to me the power that's unleashed when we approach others without masks, unvarnished, relying solely on God's redemptive work in our lives rather than our own mimicry of perfection. The thrill of intimacy with a group of women half a world away will be with me always. By stepping out from behind the mask, I experienced some of the best days of my life.

Since I began revealing the genuine Sandy with all her failings and weaknesses, most people I encounter connect with me to a greater degree. They feel a kinship, an attachment, a fondness for me that would not have been possible with my mask firmly in place. The perfectly veneered Sandy with her perfectly lived life encouraged very few, but the Genuine Article—the real Sandy behind the mask—offers hope and courage to those she meets.

Have I described your mask? Do you wear a mask by another name? You can determine what mask you wear by examining your behavior patterns and the motivations hidden behind them. Don't wait to find yourself weakened and in trouble before asking God to expose the mask you wear. If you struggle to experience intimacy with God, your husband, and others, ask Him to remove your mask. He will take you on a journey uniquely designed by His loving wisdom to help you become the Genuine Article.

> Am I willing to reduce myself simply to "me," determinedly to strip myself of all that my friends think of me, of all I think of myself, and to hand that simple naked self over to God? Immediately I am, He will sanctify me wholly, and my life will be free from earnestness in connection with everything but God.[5]

Living as the Genuine Article without masks requires you to do things differently: to find your strength in God, admit your imperfections, forgive those who've offended you, and say "no" more often. It allows you to have greater intimacy with your husband and others, show hospitality, and give to those in need. Most importantly, living as the Genuine Article, you will experience intimacy with God—and that will impact your marriage and your world.

Reflection

1. With which mask do you most identify: Superwoman, Material Girl, Perfect Ten, or another?
2. Do you feel safer behind a mask? Why or why not?
3. Is living behind a mask working for you? Explain.
4. Would you feel comfortable in your church if others knew of your weaknesses and failings? If not, why?
5. Have you recently shared your struggles with others in a vulnerable way? If not, why? What would it take for you to overcome your fear?
6. What is your underlying motive when trying to impress others?
7. Does the way you spend your time and money reflect God's desires or yours?

First Steps

1. Tell someone which mask you wear and practice lowering it with your close relationships or with women in your Beautiful Womanhood small group. In your prayer journal, record your thoughts and feelings about doing so.

2. Talk with your husband about the type of mask you've worn and why you've worn it. Ask him how, if in any way, it has affected your marriage. Journal about his response and your reaction. Alert him of your need for encouragement to lower and remove the mask.

CHAPTER FOUR

Cultivating Mystique

❧

For we are God's masterpiece. He has created us anew in Christ
Jesus, so that we can do the good things He planned for us long ago.
—EPHESIANS 2:10

Embrace the mystery of all you can be.
—MICHAEL W. SMITH

What is mystique? The dictionary defines it as "an air of mystery and reverence developing around someone."[1] Dr. James Dobson has said, "A woman who has mystique has a certain belief in her worth, in her position, in her personality, and in her relationships."[2] Bottom line, mystique is the result of inner confidence.

The husband of a confident woman is blessed! He can relax in her presence rather than work overtime to reassure her of her worth. He benefits from the value she adds to his life as she grows and flourishes within the many roles she holds. He rejoices in her special beauty that first attracted him. He also has the opportunity to enjoy godly, healthy relationships outside the marriage because his wife isn't a vacuum of neediness sucking all his attention. A good man is captivated by a woman who is confident, secure, and loves the socks off him!

How do we develop an air of mystery and reverence? Is it possible to cultivate belief in our worth, position, personality, and relationships? Yes! When you focus on the four traits of mystique—assurance, advancement, appearance, and attitude—your inner confidence will bloom.

ASSURANCE

A woman of mystique possesses an assurance of her worth, and is not plagued by insecurities. Do you struggle with feelings of low self-worth? In the past, I often found myself discouraged and frustrated with my relationships with others. I didn't realize my poor self-image was causing me to feel inadequate as a wife, mother, and friend. In my head, I kept hearing the message: "I am good enough—until someone better comes along." I was convinced it was only a matter of time before that happened.

I recall the episode that planted that lie in my heart. Marilyn was my best friend in fourth grade. We did everything together, including staying overnight at each other's house. In fifth grade, two girls began including Marilyn in their circle—excluding me. Marilyn walked out of my life, and I never understood why. Through that painful experience, Satan planted the lie in my heart that I was only good enough until someone better came along.

This lie became the filter through which I perceived life. After this, I encountered many other painful experiences that reinforced the lie I already believed. Because I believed that I wasn't good enough, I experienced hurt in situations even when none was intended.

Reject the Lies

What negative messages echo through your mind? Many people, including Christians, do not realize the tactics of our enemy, Satan. In John 10:10, Jesus says that Satan's "purpose is to steal and kill and destroy." I have found that the possession Satan wants most to steal from us is the knowledge of our identity in Christ. In other words, he wants to steal, kill, and destroy our conviction of how deeply God values us now that we're His adopted children. Satan knows we are tremendously valued by God, and he fears the day we believe it. He pummels us with negative messages concerning our worth, brainwashing us to keep us from the truth.

The only way to be truly self-assured—to possess the inner confidence and mystique that alludes so many—is to know how deeply the Father loves you. If you have accepted Jesus Christ as your Lord and Savior, you can break free from Satan's lies and discover the truth about who you really are.

You were created to be a one-of-a-kind reflection of God. No one else bears His image quite like you do. You are so deeply and passionately loved and valued by God that He sent His only son Jesus to die for you, to rescue you from Satan, and to bring you into His home. He did this so that, in the ages to come, He could shower upon you the immeasurable riches of His kindnesses. The King of the Universe wants you to be His precious bride for all time.

Unfortunately, too many of us have memorized these truths but never understood them with our hearts. The apostle Paul knew how critical it is for us to understand and experience God's great love for us, so we can know it in our minds and feel it in our hearts. That's why he prayed,

> May your roots go down deep into the soil of God's marvelous love. And may you have the power to understand, as all God's people should, how wide, how long, how high, and how deep his love really is. May you experience the love of Christ, though it is so great you will never fully understand it. Then you will be filled with the fullness of life and power that comes from God. (Ephesians 3:17–19)

When you see yourself in the mirror of your past, remembering what others have said about you or other negative experiences, you live in defeat. When you see yourself in the mirror of God's love and His Word, you find assurance of your great worth and you can experience an abundant life.

Listen to the Truth

Satan will continue to demean you with negative messages until you accept God's truth about yourself. As you feed yourself daily from

God's Word, "let God transform you into a new person by changing the way you think" (Romans 12:2)—God will rewire your thinking.

Speak aloud the following verses, and any others you find that encourage you, every day. This is the voice of truth!

+ I am loved by God (Ephesians 2:4).
+ Nothing can separate me from His love (Romans 8:38).
+ He chose me (Ephesians 1:4).
+ God bought me at a high price (1 Corinthians 6:20).
+ I am His masterpiece created in Christ Jesus for good works (Ephesians 2:10).
+ I can be victorious through Christ who loves me (Romans 8:37).
+ God's mighty power works within me to accomplish abundantly more than I could ask, think, hope, or imagine (Ephesians 3:20).

This is what God says about you. If you don't believe Him, you are calling God a liar! You can be assured through God's Word that your worth is immeasurable. As you learn from His Word, your confidence will bud as you see yourself through God's eyes. Assurance of what your Father God thinks of you is the foundation of inner confidence.

Even as I've grown in assurance, sometimes I'm tempted to become possessive of my friends when we are among other women, fearing that I'm not good enough. However, in those times I reject the enemy's lie, and I don't question my worth. Instead I speak my Father's words concerning me, and I experience His love, acceptance, and peace.

A woman of mystique will find assurance of her worth as she spends time in the presence of the mighty God who loves her dearly.

ADVANCEMENT

Once you realize you are an amazing woman with immense potential, surrounded by God's love, you will discover within you the courage to step into the adventures God has planned for you. *Advancement* is all about fulfilling the plans that the Lord has for you.

I have long dreamed of writing and becoming a published author, but my journey of advancement didn't start there. It began by digging into Scripture when I was desperate to learn what God required of me in the midst of an emotional and verbally abusive marriage. Obeying His Word and receiving godly counsel and mentoring, I was able to reverse negative behavioral patterns that had plagued me for years. These changes ushered healing into my life and God used them as a catalyst for healing in my husband and marriage. Eager to share what I learned with others, I began teaching at church. This sparked a desire to become a better speaker, which led me to take a course on speaking. It was at the speaking class where I was encouraged to begin writing about marriage. God will work out His plans for your life step by step as you advance.

To cultivate your mystique through advancement, begin by uncovering your passions and considering the season. Then move forward by making time and maintaining priorities.

Uncover Your Passions

What brings you deep gladness? What needs are you motivated to fill? In what area of your life has God done something so amazing that you just have to share it with others?

When my children were young, I made the choice to homeschool them. Creating lesson plans, planning field trips, and encouraging my kids' dancing and musical abilities became my passion. I was glad (most days) to have my children home with me, and I was motivated to fill this need.

Now, my passion is the Beautiful Womanhood ministry. God has done so much in my life and marriage that I want to share all I have learned with others so that they don't have to make the same mistakes I did. I feel God's call to this place where my passion and the world's hunger meet. As I step out courageously, "the Lord will fulfill his purpose for me" (Psalm 138:8 NIV).

One biblical example of an advancing woman is found in Proverbs 31. The woman described there clearly loved fabric, and she worked hard at creating it: "She finds wool and flax and busily spins it. . . . She quilts her own bedspreads. She dresses like royalty in gowns of finest cloth. . . . She makes belted linen garments and sashes to sell to the merchants" (verses 13, 22, 24). Her passion for gardening caused her to be on the lookout for a great piece of property: "She goes out to inspect a field and buys it; with her earnings she plants a vineyard" (verse 16). Her passions took her in many directions, and she eventually realized her goals. This woman had uncovered her passions and was about the business of developing them.

As this woman advanced, it deeply affected her husband. He praised her and said, "There are many virtuous and capable women in the world, but you surpass them all!" (verse 29). He was impressed by all she accomplished. He was fascinated by her.

Deborah, a Beautiful Womanhood marriage mentor, shares her story of advancement:

> I have a great passion for reading. Years ago, I had a strong desire to become a better wife and mother, and I found the help I needed in the Bible and Christian self-help books. I read everything I could get my hands on. Reading allowed me to grow and become a better wife and mother.
>
> Now, I pass on what I have learned through my study of God's Word, good books, and practical experience to help others become better wives and mothers. I mentor many women one-on-one and during Beautiful Womanhood small groups.

Deborah is a dynamic woman of God, confident in her place in the body of Christ, and she is being used by God. Like He did with her, God will use your passions to bless others.

You may be at a loss as to just *what* your passions are and/or *how* they might connect to the plans God has for you. Christian life-coaches can be very helpful in that case. I've worked with a life coach and have experienced numerous and wonderful benefits as a result. Life coaches help you flourish in work, life, and relationships; reach your God-given potential; overcome your challenges; and become all God has designed you to be.

Consider the Season

Different times and seasons of life affect our passions. When my children were small, I focused on my passion to see them be all they could be. Now that my children are grown, I am able to focus on my passion to help women be all they can be. God didn't pass me by during the years I was ministering to my children and taking care of my home. He was preparing me for the next step of advancement.

If you have young children, finding the time to uncover and develop your other passions can be difficult. Have patience while your children grow and until your circumstances change. God has a plan for your life; He will fulfill it. As you advance where you're placed, God will use you in ways you would never have imagined.

If you work outside the home, you are already building mystique by advancing. In this season of life, you might not have the time to pursue all your passions, but your husband will be grateful for and proud of your contribution to the family. No matter what type of work you do, think about how you can add your own special touch to the job. You can be "the aroma of Christ among those who are being saved and those who are perishing" (2 Corinthians 2:15 NIV).

Make Time

One of the key ingredients of advancement is time. Because most of us lead hectic lives, you may not have much—or any—free time. If this is the case, you might need to use time previously devoted to other things in order to begin pursuing your passions.

For one week, keep track of the activities that you're involved in and the time each takes. Evaluate whether or not you could be spending your time more wisely. Are there any TV programs that you could eliminate? Could you shorten your time online? On the phone? How much time would this free up for you to actively begin pursuing your passions?

If you have young children, plan to invest a small amount of time while they are napping or watching a favorite television show or video. You may have time to only read a little about the area of your passion, but that's a great place to start. You'll be laying the groundwork for future endeavors.

Maintain Priorities

Maintaining proper priorities is very important to uncovering your passions and developing them. Your mystery, your mystique, will soon fade if you forsake your priorities in favor of your passions.

God, your husband, and your children should be your top priorities—in that order, followed by your passion. We neglect God, our first priority, when we chase our passion to the exclusion of Him. This is possible even when our passion is ministry. Martha was so busy serving Jesus, she forgot the "one thing" God most desires: drawing near to Him (see Luke 10:38–42).

Is your husband supportive of your passion? If not, ask him why and listen carefully to his feedback. Don't respond right away, but tell him you appreciate his thoughts and will think about what he's said. Take some time to prayerfully consider his objections. In a true partnership, contrary opinions aren't an excuse to dismiss the other person. There must be a reason for his concern. Get to the bottom of that concern, and you will discover more about yourself and your husband. If you still don't agree with your husband's original assessment, tell him you've considered his thoughts and would like to revisit the discussion. "God is not the author of confusion but of peace" (1 Corinthians 14:33 NKJV); He wouldn't ask you to submit to your husband and then tell you to proceed with a passion your husband isn't in favor of. Listen to what God is telling you through His Word and prayer.

When the Lord first placed the vision for the Beautiful Womanhood ministry in my heart, I literally gushed about Beautiful Womanhood. I thought about Beautiful Womanhood during the day and dreamed about it at night. Whenever Tom and I were alone, I'd talk about Beautiful Womanhood. It didn't matter what we would start talking about, I'd always bring the topic back to Beautiful Womanhood. I didn't listen to Tom as I had in the past—I was intent on talking about my passion. In all honesty, I was obnoxious! Passion that neglects priorities isn't beautiful.

After my first seminar, Tom suggested I take a week off to recover from all the study and preparations that had consumed me for so long. I was rather annoyed that he felt it necessary for me to take a break. I actually wondered if he was trying to stand in the way of my progress for the Lord. My attitude was causing a lot of tension between us.

I decided to drop my defenses long enough to see if he had a point, so I took the week off. It became clear that my home had become a sacrifice on the altar of Beautiful Womanhood. Many of my responsibilities in the home had been neglected, and I wasn't showing respect to Tom as I made everything about me. The Beautiful Womanhood ministry is a good thing, but it's not more important than obeying God and honoring my husband. I had forsaken many priorities in favor of my passion.

I was surprised to find that the Proverbs 31 woman, as focused on advancement as she was, seemed to be deliberate about maintaining her priorities. The passage recounts her efforts to get up early in order to feed her family (verse 15), to shop for bargains (verse 18), to reach out to those less fortunate (verse 20), and to keep her family clothed (verse 21). She had her eye on everything that was going on under her roof, and worked hard to care for it (verse 27). Her passions did not surpass her priorities. Because of this her husband and children praise her: "There are many virtuous and capable women in the world, but you surpass them all!" (verse 29).

The Lord will never ask you to sacrifice your priorities to follow your passion. He is not a God of confusion; He is a God of peace. If your family members are often left to fend for themselves, if there is tension between you and your husband, or if there is a lack of peace in your home, something is out of balance. Lay your passion aside long enough to determine what is causing strife in your home. If damage occurs in your family, no amount of success in your passion will make up for it. Maintaining your priorities ensures your advance won't be temporary. Finding balance between your priorities and passions may take some work, but seek peace and you will find it.

Do you believe that God had amazing plans in mind when He created you? When you focus on learning new things—advancement—you begin to discover ways in which you can fulfill all that the Lord has planned for you. Psalm 138:8 says, "The LORD will work out his plans for my life—for your faithful love, O LORD, endures forever."

APPEARANCE

Some women may balk at the suggestion that *appearance* plays an important role in cultivating our mystique and strengthening our relationship with our husband. However, it would be unwise to ignore the evidence to the contrary.

Why is appearance important for developing mystique? Let me answer that question with another. Do you have more confidence when you look your best? Of course you do. Jill Krieger Swanson says, "Clothing and appearance affect how we feel and think about ourselves. They can lift our spirits and help give us confidence to face the real world."[3] When we look and feel our best, it does wonders for our self-confidence, and that's what mystique is all about.

While looking our best makes us feel more confident, there is a second reason for maintaining a good appearance. Men are visual. Shaunti Feldhahn's book, *For Women Only: What You Need to Know About the Inner Lives of Men*, reveals how important appearance is to our husbands. "Since men are so visual," she writes, "seeing us make the effort to look good makes them feel loved and cared for."[4] When Feldhahn conducted a survey, seven out of ten men indicated that they would be emotionally bothered if the woman in their life let herself go and didn't seem to want to make the effort to do something about it.[5]

One reason your husband married you was because you were attractive to him. You loved it that he was attracted to you while you were dating. And you probably spent some time, energy, and resources (he had no idea how much) to make sure he stayed attracted to you. The benefits of that kind of investment will continue to pay dividends! Making the effort to look good will improve your relationship with your husband—thus giving you more confidence and mystique.

Define Your Style

What style makes you look and feel great?

We are all individuals; our individuality should shine through our style. I have enjoyed talking with many women about who they are, from the inside out. The words you use to describe your personality can also be used to identify your personal style. When you look in your closet and examine your lifestyle, which clothes best reflect your personality?

I hope you'll come up with your own term that defines your personal style. I know several women who have done this, and it's lots of fun! Allow these to stir your creativity:

- ✦ Classic Comfort
- ✦ Chic Boutique
- ✦ Urban Glamour
- ✦ Classic Vintage

- ✦ Earthy Bohemian
- ✦ Natural Romance
- ✦ Vivid Whimsy
- ✦ Soulful Nouveau

Because you are a unique creation of God, the sky's the limit when defining your own personal style.

In the movie, *What a Girl Wants*, a young man says to the girl he loves, "Why try so hard to fit in when you were born to stand out?"[6] Finding and developing your unique mystique will cause you to stand out in confidence.

Consider Angela, a woman involved in a Beautiful Womanhood small group, who writes:

> My whole life, when I looked in the mirror, I saw an ugly woman. I would compare myself with everyone. This wore me out. My husband would tell me that I was beautiful, but I couldn't absorb the compliment. I'd tell him that he was under contract to say that! Now, when I look in the mirror, I feel beautiful. I have my own style. For the first time in my life I feel comfortable being me! This has been the most life-changing lesson for me.

Angela has developed her own personal style, and her self-confidence has soared.

A focus on appearance in order to gain self-confidence shouldn't pressure you into becoming someone you're not, but is meant to help you discover how best to express who you already are. If you haven't thought about this before, the process of developing a personal style that reveals your unique self may take some time.

It's important you avoid the pitfall of building a mystique-inspired wardrobe overnight. Discovering your personal style should not be used as an excuse for abusing your budget or spending plan. Take your time and begin by adding basic pieces to your wardrobe and, as your budget allows, embellish your wardrobe with items consistent with your personal style. Overall, discovering your unique mystique has the potential to keep more pennies in your pocketbook. You won't be as quick to succumb to impulsive purchases or spending to keep up with trends. Any investment you make should be intentional. Remember, it's not about perfection according to the world's standards but about finding and enhancing your uniqueness. Enjoy!

Consider His Preference

In addition to figuring out your own personal style, it's also important to consider your husband's preference regarding your appearance. In the Bible, when Esther was vying for the position of queen, "she accepted the advice of Hegai, the eunuch in charge of the harem. She asked for nothing except what he suggested, and she was admired by everyone who saw her" (Esther 2:15). Hegai knew the king better than anyone, and she was wise to consult him. Taking his advice helped her win the crown. Considering your husband's input will help you win his admiration.

One woman asked me for advice because her husband liked to see her in suits, but she didn't care for them. I suggested she wear them on an occasional Sunday, for special occasions, or when going out on a date with him. I'm not suggesting that you become someone else's ideal, but, when it comes to your husband, try to incorporate his preferences. If you dress in professional wear but your husband prefers some pizzazz, wear undergarments with pizzazz. Your personal style is still prominent, but he will appreciate the just-for-me efforts you make. Accessorize with his favorite color; wear a cologne that he has commented on; build an outfit around a piece of jewelry that he bought for you.

I've had other young women tell me their husband wanted them to dress immodestly for them in public. You should not dress in a provocative way in public, even to entice your husband. However, after you put your kids to bed, you can slip into something that will invite him to pursue you. If you strike that balance—if he knows that you're willing to seduce him—he will be more understanding when you explain why you don't dress in such a way in public that might encourage others to lust.

ATTITUDE

The fourth focus of mystique is *attitude*. A woman of mystique develops good attitudes toward her husband, toward others, and toward herself. Positive attitudes improve relationships and improved relationships give us more confidence. Encouragement, discretion, and courage are three key attitudes that all women should seek to grow in.

Encouragement

A woman with inner confidence is able to encourage her husband and others because she is self-assured. When you are self-assured, you have the energy to focus on others because it isn't all drained away focusing on yourself. Is your husband discouraged? Are there areas of his life needing a healthy dose of encouragement?

You can't give what you don't possess, so it is vital that you receive the encouragement God gives through His Word in order to give it away. I keep a list of verses containing promises I come across in my daily Bible reading, and I record them in a journal for easy access when Tom needs encouragement. I encourage him with God's Word.

When Tom is feeling low, I also encourage him by calling out the strengths and talents I see in his life. This encouragement is a sustaining factor when he struggles with difficult issues. He is grateful for my belief in him and I feel good knowing I've spoken honest, life-giving, positive words during troubled times. Some of a woman's mystery is found in her deep thoughtfulness. She is tuned in to the needs of her husband and is willing to give him the encouragement he so desperately needs.

When you are a positive force in others' lives, it enhances mystique. "Those who refresh others will themselves be refreshed" (Proverbs 11:25). Knowing you are making a difference in their lives "refreshes" you, and increases your inner confidence.

Discretion

Proverbs 11:22 says, "A woman who is beautiful but lacks discretion is like a gold ring in a pig's snout." The dictionary defines *discretion* as a cautious reserve in speech.[7] Caution isn't something many of us exercise in regard to our communication with our husband, but we should.

A woman of mystique recognizes that her husband may not think or communicate like her, so she will exercise discretion. One of the wisest people who ever lived wrote, "There is a time for everything . . . a time to be silent and a time to speak" (Ecclesiastes 3:1, 7 NIV). I may prefer to discuss schedules and issues first thing in the morning, but I am not married to a morning person, so I have learned (and am still learning) to use discretion when I speak. Tom may not have noticed my improved sense of timing, but I know that it has prepared the way for more effective communication with him.

You may want to unload all the day's happenings on your husband as soon as you see each other in the evening, but your husband might prefer a chance to unwind before going over your list of things to discuss. A question I ask myself before telling something to my husband is, *Am I about to regurgitate everything that I've experienced during the day?* Like Tom, maybe your husband will appreciate you saving certain details for your girlfriends.

Speaking of details, a woman of mystique does not gossip about others. Do you put others down in order to feel better about yourself? Filling a need for affirmation that way is incompatible with mystique. If you are sharing confidential or personal information that *you* wouldn't want shared with others, don't do it—even with your husband. This destroys mystique. There is no mystery to a woman who has a loose mouth. Everyone knows what she thinks about everything.

Be watchful about the things you say. May others say of you what David said of Abigail, "Blessed be your discretion, and blessed be you" (1 Samuel 25:33 RSV).

Courage

A courageous woman is not afraid to learn and grow as an individual. Many women defeat themselves in their own minds before ever attempting anything new. In what area are you in need of courage?

When I was a young wife, I was very shy about meeting new people. Whenever we were invited to a gathering with people I didn't know, I'd beg Tom to stay home because my inner confidence was low. I was focused on the fact that I was shy around new people and didn't make friends easily. This kept me from achieving anything different than what I believed about myself. Proverbs 29:25 exposed my wrong thinking: "Fearing people is a dangerous trap, but to trust the LORD means safety."

I have learned that you have to face your fear in order to dispel it, pressing past the thing you fear doing and "do it afraid" as Joyce Meyer says.[8] I like the way the Amplified Bible translates Philippians 4:13: "I am ready for anything and equal to anything through Him Who infuses inner strength into me." It's true! With God's help, His strength in me is enough to do the very thing I fear. When I press past my fear and "do it afraid," I find that the fear itself was much worse than the action I feared doing. President Franklin D. Roosevelt's words ring true: "The only thing we have to fear is fear itself."[9]

I now meet new women everywhere I speak, and it's one of my favorite aspects of ministry. I've learned the art of interacting one-on-one with new people, and it is a tremendous blessing. And as it has added to my inner confidence, it has added to my mystique.

Offering encouragement, practicing discretion, and having courage will do wonders for building your mystique. You will be surprised at how your inner confidence grows as you embrace these attitudes.

Becoming a woman of mystique is a lifelong process—there is nothing "instant" about it. I have certainly grown in mystique as the years have passed, although I often felt that the progress was excruciatingly slow. For the most part, I have grown one step at a time—not fully realizing where God was leading. Looking back, I am amazed at how a series of small steps became a journey to new and exciting places. That's one of the joys of growing older.

Begin now to develop your *assurance, advancement, appearance,* and *attitudes* that will bring about inner confidence in your worth, your position, your personality, and your relationships.

Enjoy the journey as you grow in mystique.

——————————— *Reflection* ———————————

1. What phrase often plays in your mind and undermines your belief in yourself? Where did it come from: your past, your experiences, or what other people said about you? Does it agree with God's Word?

2. Imagine deleting that repeating phrase and inserting what God says about you instead. If you did that, how would it affect your choices and your relationship with your husband?

3. What dreams or ideas have you thought about over the years? Which ones would you like to advance in? Is now a good season for advancing? If not, when might be?

4. What is one small action you could take to set yourself on the path of that advancement process?

5. Consider the pattern of your life. What do your actions show are your priorities?

6. What do you like about your personality? Your appearance? What words would you use to describe your personality and thus your personal style?

7. Where do you try to "fit in" rather than embrace your true self? What steps can you take to express your individuality?

8. What area of discretion—timing, details, or gossip—is most difficult for you? Why?

9. Do you seek opportunities to be a force of encouragement in your husband's life? How has this affected him?

——————————— *First Steps* ———————————

1. Keep a running list of verses that describe how God feels about you and write them in your prayer journal.

2. Uncover one or two passions in your life and record them

in your prayer journal. Write in your journal a plan for advancing them when the time is right.

3. Discuss your ideas of *advancement* with your husband. Share with him how the *assurance* of how God sees you has made an impact on your life. Ask his input concerning your *appearance*.

CHAPTER FIVE

Inviting Romance

In quietness and confidence is your strength.
—ISAIAH 30:15

*At some core place, maybe deep within, perhaps hidden
or buried in her heart, every woman wants to be seen,
wanted, and pursued. We want to be romanced.*
—JOHN AND STASI ELDREDGE, *CAPTIVATING*

*E*nvision your husband wrapping his arms around you from behind and whispering in your ear, "You're amazing," or stealing you away for dinner at your favorite restaurant (he made babysitting arrangements), or holding your hand while taking a walk, or ringing your doorbell only to present you with a bouquet of your favorite flowers. What fans the embers of romance deep within your heart?

Most women dream of romance but many don't consider how their words or actions might be dousing the passion in their marriages. Are your words and actions stumbling blocks or invitations to your husband to join you in a romantic relationship?

Have you ever heard the saying, "If you do what you've always done, you'll get what you've always gotten"? This saying rings true in regards to romance. Reflect a moment on the results of your actions and words and ask yourself, "Do I like what I'm getting?"

If you desire more romance, you must change your actions and trace a new path for your feet. Hebrews 12:13 says, "Mark out a straight path for your feet. Then those who follow you, though they are weak and lame, will not stumble and fall but will become strong."

Using the acronym TRACE, let's look at five steps you can take to change your actions and invite your husband into greater romance.

Trust instead of control

Respect instead of demean

Appreciate instead of criticize

Confer confidence instead of doubt

Expose vulnerability instead of defensiveness

Through these steps, you can *trace* a new path for your feet and provide your husband the safety and encouragement he needs to set foot upon the path of a more romantic marriage.

TRUST INSTEAD OF CONTROL

Do you struggle with a desire to control those around you? Most women, including myself, wrestle with control issues. The desire to control our husbands is a result of sin. After Eve and Adam disobeyed God in the garden of Eden, God told Eve, "You will bear children with intense pain and suffering. *And though your desire will be for your husband*, he will be your master" (Genesis 3:16, emphasis mine). The Hebrew word *tesuqah*, translated here as "desire," means "desire to overcome or defeat another."[1]

To get a sense of whether you have control issues in your marriage, ask yourself these questions: Do I correct my husband? Do I instruct my husband? Do I try to improve my husband?

I have been guilty of all three!

Correcting Your Husband

I am engaged in a never-ending struggle to stop correcting my husband (and others). My tendency to correct shows itself most often in the area of pronunciation. Every time Tom mispronounces a word,

I pipe up with the correct pronunciation, and if he stumbles over a word, I'm there to pick him up, dust him off, and set him on his feet again. It's a knee-jerk reaction.

Tom doesn't appreciate my corrections. They point out the fact that he isn't doing something right. Most men don't appreciate this kind of exposure. Unless your husband asks for your help, spotlighting his mistakes robs you of romance with him—the very thing you desire.

Instructing Your Husband

A young woman once asked me if it was right to instruct her husband in how to bathe their baby. She had asked him for more help with the kids, and one evening he offered to give the baby a bath. Things were going smoothly until she heard crying coming from the bathroom. She flew into the bathroom; shampoo was in the baby's eyes, and Dad was working frantically to get it out. Mom stepped in to save the day, instructing Dad in how to do the job.

I asked her, "Did he ask for your help?"

"No."

"Do you think he will offer to bathe the baby again anytime soon?"

"No."

"Was this the result you wanted?"

"No."

She had probably married a bright man who could figure out how to handle their baby's eye irritation and how to avoid that happening next time. She could have waited until he had finished and thanked him for helping her. She could have given him a big hug and thanked him for being a great dad. This would have given her what she wanted—help with the kids and an opportunity to prove her trust in him. In turn, this would have made him feel appreciated and loved—fertile soil for the seeds of romance.

Improving Your Husband

One evening while on vacation, my husband and I decided to go to a nice restaurant. I dressed in a black, vintage cashmere jacket with a white blouse, silk scarf, and heels. Tom chose black hiking shoes, khaki zip-off pants, and a wrinkled white camp shirt—complete with mesh vents for proper ventilation, plenty of Velcro, and loops and snaps for holding everything from compasses to ice-picks. The frosting on the cake came in the form of the yellow silk tie he had just bought. I was taking it all in when he proudly announced, "I'm ready to go!"

I didn't say a word about Tom's appearance—you can appreciate what restraint that took—because I know something that I didn't know years ago: men do not like to be improved by their wives. My husband was pleased with his appearance; it reflected the playfulness he felt. He would never dress this way for a business meeting or other formal event, but on vacation his outfit could express his fun-loving nature. Any attempt to improve Tom's attire would have been met with resistance, not romance.

Relinquish Control—Trust God

When you correct your husband, you're saying, "You didn't do it right." When you instruct your husband, you're saying, "You don't know how to do it." When you improve your husband, you're saying, "You didn't do it well enough." As Dr. Ed Cole suggests, when you tell your husband what to do, you become his mother, and a man can't make love to his mother![2]

We justify our actions by telling ourselves that we're just trying to help our husband, but our motives may have more to do with control than help. Control is often rooted in fear. Some women try to control their husband out of fear that they won't get what they want. Others fear their husband's actions will reflect badly upon them if they don't step in to "help." At the root of our fear is selfishness, and selfishness does not serve as an invitation to romance. Philippians 2:3 says, "Don't be selfish; don't live to make a good impression on others."

You come from a long line of women who would rather control than trust. If you go back to the very beginning, you see how Eve

Inviting Romance

distrusted God and took control. God had placed Adam and Eve in a beautiful garden. He said they could eat from every tree except the tree of the knowledge of good and evil—or they'd die. The serpent deceived Eve, telling her she wouldn't die, but her eyes would be opened and she would know good and evil, becoming like God. Afraid that she was missing out, Eve took control; she ate the fruit and gave some to her husband. Eve was convinced that God was withholding something from her. "When Eve was convinced," writes Jan Meyers, "the artistry of being a woman took a fateful dive into the barren places of control and loneliness."[3]

What is there about the nature of control that blocks romance and intimacy? The best way to answer this question is with another question. Do you want to get close to a controlling person? No, of course not. It's impossible to experience intimacy when controls are placed on you. Your husband feels the same way. So, if you want to increase the romance in your marriage, it's time to trust God and let go of control.

How, exactly? It's simple, but it's not easy: expose your fear, repent, and turn to God when you feel an urge to control. For example, I corrected Tom's pronunciation because I was afraid people might think *I* didn't know the correct pronunciation if I didn't step in. In order to stop this self-defeating action, I had to turn to God and admit my fear and control, understand that it's not my role to correct Tom, and rely on the community of women around me for encouragement and accountability.

"Give all your worries and cares to God, for he cares about what happens to you" (1 Peter 5:7). Telling God my worries is easy; giving them to Him—and leaving them in His hands—takes practice. I often pray, "God, if his behavior is bothering you half as much as it's bothering me, would you please do something!" Most of the time, God isn't that bothered, and I'm challenged to keep still. When I let God be in charge of instructing my husband, I'm free to enjoy Tom for who he is.

Controlling, instructing, and improving your husband carry him

93

back to his boyhood, and little boys do not walk the path of romance. Trusting your husband will invite him to romance.

RESPECT INSTEAD OF DEMEAN

In my twenties, whenever I blew out my birthday candles, I wished for the same thing: I wanted to respect my husband more. I had read it in the Bible: "Each man must love his wife as he loves himself, and the wife must respect her husband" (Ephesians 5:33). Unfortunately, I didn't enjoy any consistency on this point. While the candle smoke wafted upward, I sat back, crossed my arms, and waited for Tom to do something that I could fully respect.

What was wrong? I thought I needed Tom to inspire me to take the action of respecting him. Instead, I needed to obey God and take the first step toward respect. It has been said that it is easier to act yourself into a new way of thinking than to think yourself into a new way of acting. We would be wise to adopt Nike's motto and "Just do it!"

What motivates our disrespect of our husbands? Some of us play tit for tat—"You don't give me love, so I won't give you respect." Others think disrespect will motivate our husbands—"When you give me love, I'll give you respect." Some of us grew up watching our mother disrespect our father and are simply well trained. Others of us hope to increase our own low self-esteem by demeaning our husbands—using disrespect as a weapon in a one-sided battle for what we perceive as the only safe place in the household: the top. Pride can also trigger disrespect, when we forget that our way is not the only way to do something and we start thinking, *I know better than he does.*

Unless we stop our disrespectful ways and choose to start respecting our husbands, our best chance for romance lies only in our dreams.

Consider the Chickens' Way

We live on a small farm, and since we added chickens to our stock, the term "pecking order" has taken on new meaning for me.

Shortly after establishing them in their coop, we witnessed harassment, chicken-style. The dominant chickens chose a chicken to chase and peck. Every time it went near the feeder, they chased it all over the coop—keeping it from the food it needed for survival.

It didn't take long to determine which chicken was at the bottom of the pecking order. It was the one with missing feathers and patches of puffy, bloody skin. When one of our chickens looked like this, it was only a matter of time before we found it dead on the floor of the coop.

Ever hear the term "hen-pecked husband"? A hen-pecked husband is usually at the bottom of the pecking order in the home. When you emasculate your husband to this condition, you reduce him to a state that is no longer respectable. You have become your own worst enemy because you truly want a respectable husband. You thought you were helping elevate your husband to higher and higher levels of manhood, but, in reality, you were diminishing him. His place is now at the bottom of the pecking order of your home, and he isn't able to get what he needs for survival: respect.

Consider Your Husband's Ways

Your husband won't always tell you he feels emasculated or wounded when you demean or disrespect him. He may step back and allow you to lead rather than fight for control. He may shrink from becoming the man God intended him to be if he fears your disrespectful, sarcastic attitude. The negative message you transmit undermines what he already questions in his heart—his worth as a man.

Or perhaps when your husband feels disrespected he speaks harshly to you or undermines you. It becomes a game of matching strength for strength in order to preserve any semblance of self-respect—no matter how shredded.

What does respect have to do with intimacy and romance? When a man is confident in your opinion of him, he can relax with you. He can drop his walls and let you in. He knows that with you, he is safe.

He will be valued and respected. And where there is safety, intimacy can grow.

APPRECIATE INSTEAD OF CRITICIZE

It is often easier to be dissatisfied and critical instead of appreciative. Consider the following story sent to me by a young wife:

> Just yesterday we were discussing the repair bill on our van and how we were going to cover it. It seems to be an impossible necessity! The not-so-beautiful little girl in me wanted to get angry, stomp, scream, cry, and blame my husband for not taking care of the little issues that continually seem to crop up. I felt his procrastination had caused this seemingly insurmountable repair bill, and I was convinced I had ample reasons for being dissatisfied over how he was handling it. I have learned, however, that he is perfectly capable of beating himself up and doesn't need my help doing so. I knew he would clam up and retreat inside himself if I blamed him. So, I chose instead to honor my husband, in order to avoid days of the cold silent treatment.
>
> While awaiting his return from work, I listed in my mind all the amazing ways he provides for us, the hours he works so I can stay home with our children, and how he comes home happy and helpful to us after long days. I became so filled with appreciation that there was no longer any room for dissatisfaction.
>
> In the grand scheme of life, what is a little repair bill? Our marriage is strong, but it could suffer damage if I let this bill take priority. It's not worth it! I truly believe that when I react in the proper way toward my husband, God rewards me. In this situation, I made a choice to go to my husband with an attitude of appreciation, praising him for being a hard worker and provider and reassuring him that everything would be fine. He needed my support and encouragement, not my dissatisfac-

tion. Our relationship did not suffer, our intimacy has not been diminished, and God will supply the need!

Can you relate to the internal dilemma this wife describes? When stressed, do you focus on appreciating your husband or being dissatisfied with him? Your choice could make the difference between romance and remorse.

What does your husband do (or not do) that causes you disdain? Is it his paycheck? Is it how he performs tasks for you? Is it what he gives you or how he surprises you? I know women whose husbands have given them gifts from small trinkets to expensive jewelry, but because it wasn't exactly what they wanted, they returned it. I have done this, too.

If a man feels unappreciated—if he feels your continual dissatisfaction—he may give up trying to please you and will begin looking for other opportunities that will satisfy his need for appreciation. Are you willing to risk this when the desire of most good men is to satisfy their wives?

As most women have experienced, the male ego is fragile. Your husband may come off with bravado, but inside he's looking for your affirmation and appreciation. Most men can't live without it and will seek validation wherever they can find it. Let your words of appreciation be something your husband can rely on.

Keep a running list of your husband's positive traits and actions. It will help you in those moments when you are annoyed with, irritated by, or wanting to blame your husband; simply running through that list will remind you how much more there is to him than his aggravating tendency to come home late. As Paul instructs us, "Fix your thoughts on what is true and honorable and right. Think about things that are pure and lovely and admirable. Think about things that are excellent and worthy of praise" (Philippians 4:8).

Focusing on the negatives will leave you dissatisfied. Appreciating your man will invite him to romance.

CONFER CONFIDENCE INSTEAD OF DOUBT

Men are highly sensitive to signals of doubt because doubt plagues them. If you continually give off signals of doubt, you will confirm the fear of inadequacy that lurks deep within your husband. If a man believes he doesn't have what it takes to please you, there's not much chance he'll attempt romance.

"A wise woman builds her house; a foolish woman tears hers down with her own hands" (Proverbs 14:1). Doubting your husband and his abilities tears away at a man; conferring confidence builds him up. A confident man is grateful to the one who believes in him.

Do you have confidence in your husband, or do you find yourself regularly second-guessing him? Do you struggle with doubt when it comes to his abilities? He needs to be supported by your confidence in him at home, in the workplace, and in his dream for the future.

At Home

I wanted Tom involved with the discipline of our children but was rarely pleased with his methods. I thought he was too strict and should be more understanding. Instead of communicating clearly with Tom about my concerns, I undermined his authority by smoothing things over with the kids behind his back. My actions conveyed a lack of confidence in my husband. I sabotaged our parenting and our marriage. Our kids learned their parents weren't always on the same team, so if they worked on the more lenient parent, they might get their way. Tom felt hurt and angry. Doubting my husband didn't open any doors to romance.

On the Job

The media constantly broadcast fear and doubt concerning the future. Against this tidal wave of doom and gloom, it's difficult for a man to confidently believe that God has planned a hopeful future for him.

When my husband was going through a job transition a couple

of years ago, it became apparent he was struggling with doubt over his ability to succeed in a new venture. He was really down one day when he commented, "Most men don't make a job change at fifty." I asked, "Who says?" He rewarded me with a smile from ear to ear. Tom's words weren't so much a statement of fact as they were a question—he was asking me if I believed he could successfully make a job change at fifty.

A wise wife counteracts the media's message of fear with a daily dose of confidence. Inspiring confidence in your husband is like pouring water on dry, thirsty ground. What seeds of potential lie dormant within your husband, waiting for the showers of your confidence?

In His Dreams

What does your husband dream of doing? Let your husband know that you believe in him. If you don't, who will? Don't wait! Breathe words of confidence into your husband today and watch as he stands taller with every word spoken.

When considering your husband's dreams, pray about which ones to encourage. If your husband's dreams take him in a direction that worries you, consider your concerns. Are they rooted in selfishness or fear? Turn to God and give them to Him. If your concerns are motivated by love, it is important that you share them with your husband in a productive manner. Opening a dialogue allows both of you to share doubts concerning the proposed course of action. Together, pray about these doubts, asking God to reveal whether or not He is leading your husband in this direction. You have an important role in your husband's life, and it includes giving honest feedback concerning his dreams.

It won't always go smoothly when a man, inspired by his wife's confidence, explores new horizons—but that isn't the point. Your focus cannot be on his level of success but on his willingness to try. You don't always succeed when you try something new, do you? Don't set your requirements for your husband higher than you would for yourself. Check that your motives are pure. You are inspiring confidence for his benefit, not yours. Conferring confidence invites your husband to romance.

Special Note

If you are in an emotionally or physically abusive marriage, exposing your vulnerability could be damaging to you instead of healing. I urge you to seek the help you need. Contact the Domestic Abuse Hotline at 1-800-799-SAFE, or call your church and ask to be referred to a reputable Christian counselor.

EXPOSE VULNERABILITY INSTEAD OF DEFENSIVENESS

It has become second nature for women to defend themselves. For untold generations, women have been hurt, taken advantage of, and diminished in their value. With the advent of the Women's Liberation Movement, women came out swinging against the injustices they'd endured and, in the process, they lost something of great value—their vulnerability.

There is something so inviting about vulnerability. Vulnerability is armorless. Vulnerability draws others in. It invites others to look deep inside. This invitation to look inside is exactly why so many avoid vulnerability at all cost. It's dangerous.

If you offer vulnerability to your husband, what will he do with it? Hurt you? Take advantage of you? Think less of you? These risks overshadow vulnerability's beauty until you consider the consequences of a life lived defensively.

Living defensively is like living in a fortress—walls built up and weapons ready. The face behind the wall is tense, scanning for threat. A life lived on the defense is a life spent without rest, joy, or freedom. Many women dwell behind walls that inadvertently keep their husbands out, and they wonder why they do not feel known by their husbands.

Since true romance involves being known and desired, to invite your husband to romance, you must take the risk of being vulnerable, tearing down your defensive walls.

Sometimes Vulnerability Says, "I'm Hurt"

When you get hurt, do you retaliate in anger, or are you vulnerable with your husband and admit your feelings? Retaliating in anger may satisfy your thirst for justice, but it won't give you the increased romance and intimacy you want. No one approaches a fortress when arrows are flying from it—unless they are prepared for battle.

It takes more courage to admit your feelings of hurt than to defend yourself. It requires you to trust God to keep you safe when you expose your hurts, and to heal you if your husband is not gentle. The good news is that God promises to do all these things and more. Consider Psalm 91, which is a contract between God and those who trust in Him:

> Those who live in the shelter of the Most High will find rest in the shadow of the Almighty. This I declare of the LORD: He alone is my refuge, my place of safety; he is my God, and I am trusting him. . . . He will shield you with his wings. He will shelter you with his feathers. His faithful promises are your armor and protection. . . .
>
> If you make the LORD your refuge, if you make the Most High your shelter, no evil will conquer you; . . . For he orders his angels to protect you wherever you go. They will hold you with their hands to keep you from striking your foot on a stone. . . . The LORD says, "I will rescue those who love me. I will protect those who trust in my name. When they call on me, I will answer; I will be with them in trouble. I will rescue them and honor them. I will satisfy them with a long life and give them my salvation."

God wants to be your defender. When you are hurt and you retaliate in anger, you allow your sinful nature to usurp God's role, causing problems. "If your sinful nature controls your mind, there is death. But if the Holy Spirit controls your mind, there is life and peace" (Romans 8:6).

You must come to recognize what triggers you to defend yourself rather than to admit your pain. Perhaps it's a fear that your needs won't be met or that you're not valuable. When the triggers come, remind yourself that God will defend and protect you if you put your trust in Him.

Shooting arrows of anger over your walls doesn't provide your husband the safety he needs to know, desire, and pursue you. It takes courage initially to admit your feelings, but it's worth it. A better life and more peace are your rewards! Allow God to protect you and go before you, leveling your defenses and making way for your husband to romance you.

Sometimes Vulnerability Says, "I'm Not Perfect"

If your worst side was exposed, do you think you would be rejected? Does a façade give you the acceptance you long for?

Imperfection is not an attractive quality in our culture, and it is often taboo to expose imperfections. Because of this, many women cover up their flaws with a socially acceptable, yet false, exterior. How many hurting people cover up serious problems for the sake of appearance? There are no perfect people in this world, but there are many who dishonestly portray themselves as "all together."

Can anyone truly come close to being a perfect person? If you give your husband the impression that you have it all together, he will struggle with his own self-esteem in light of your seeming flawlessness. He may even distance himself from you emotionally and steer clear of revealing his true self for fear of coming up short in your estimation. Your façade may even make you less tolerant of any weaknesses your husband may show—yours have been carefully concealed, so why can't he do a better job hiding his?

A false exterior also keeps you from reaching out to God for the help you need. Unless you admit you need Him, you are keeping

God at arms' length rather than experiencing intimacy with Him and receiving help from Him.

Psalm 32:3 (NIV) says, "When I kept silent, my bones wasted away through my groaning all day long." In other words, when we refuse to confess our sins to God, we're miserable. But, when we confess them and stop trying to hide them, God forgives us and removes our guilt. We have restored intimacy with Him. I have found that I will not be rejected by God when I'm honest with Him about my problems and ask Him for help. Instead, He draws me into closer relationship.

The same is true with my husband. A false exterior keeps me from experiencing intimacy with Tom because I'm holding him at arms' length, attempting to conceal my imperfections.

Maintaining a façade to hide your weaknesses prevents your husband from knowing the real you—flaws and all. Exposing your weaknesses gives your husband the opportunity to love you as you are; this is vital for romance.

Sometimes Vulnerability Says, "You May Have a Point"

Are you open to learning from what your husband can see in you that you cannot?

Years ago, I had the opportunity to speak at a friend's church, and Tom came along to offer moral support. I taught my heart out. I was pleased with my speaking—until I asked Tom for his feedback.

My helpful husband suggested that I should try to speak with more energy and accelerate my pace. He was trying to offer a helpful critique, but the message I heard in between his words was that I wasn't a good speaker. My objections poured out; I discounted all he'd said.

Then I saw my teaching on videotape. I wanted to crawl into a hole until the pain of watching had passed. It was too slow; the energy just wasn't there.

Where had I heard that before?

I wish that I had been vulnerable with my husband by giving thought to his input when I asked for it. He would have been honored that I respected his opinion, and I would have become a better speaker earlier.

It is second nature to be defensive and thereby cut yourself off from the advantage that a second perspective brings to your life. What does your husband see in you that you cannot? Ask him. It might surprise you to hear what he has to say.

Defensiveness concerning your husband's input discredits his words. Admitting your shortcomings allows your respect of his opinion to open the door to romance. When you expose your vulnerability by admitting you're hurt, asking for his help, and respecting his perspective, you lower your defenses and invite your husband to romance.

The aspect of TRACE that I've been focusing on lately is appreciation. I have been expressing my appreciation (through laughter and words) for Tom's incredible sense of humor. His zany ways bring laughter and smiles to those he comes into contact with—even complete strangers. It's not that I didn't appreciate his sense of humor before—I love it when he makes people laugh—but sometimes I'd critique his performance and suggest he "tone it down" a bit, leaving him feeling deflated.

Since starting this intentional appreciation of my husband's sense of humor, I've noticed changes in his behavior toward me. He frequently displays many gentlemanly qualities that I really enjoy such as opening car doors, carrying heavy objects for me, holding my chair before I sit down, and allowing me to precede him when entering an elevator or room. I feel cherished when he does these things—I feel romanced!

Do your words or actions serve as stumbling blocks or invitations to your husband to join you in a romantic relationship?

1. For each of the actions listed below, think of a time when you tried to control your husband in this way. What were you afraid would happen if you let him do it his way? How did he respond to your attempts to control him?
   + Correcting
   + Instructing
   + Improving

2. In what areas do you withhold respect from your husband? What requirements must he fulfill before you give him respect? What is at the heart of your disrespect: feeling unloved, pride, low self-esteem, fear, or something else? How does your husband respond when you disrespect him?

3. Think of a time when you showed respect to your husband. How did he respond?

4. In what ways do you convey your dissatisfaction with your husband? Have you been focusing on your husband's strengths or his faults? What is one way you could show appreciation for your husband this week? Write this in your prayer journal, and after seeing your husband's response, come back and record that as well.

5. In what areas do you doubt your husband's abilities? Are these areas in which God has gifted you?

6. What self-doubt has your husband voiced? How can you express your confidence in him and boost his confidence in himself?

7. What triggers cause you to be defensive rather than vulnerable? If you don't know, ask God. Record these in your prayer journal.

8. Which areas of your life do you keep hidden because you fear rejection? With whom can you share them?

First Steps

1. Review TRACE and prayerfully determine which areas need improvement. Record them in your prayer journal. Pick one of those areas to start growing in, tell a friend, and ask her to check up on you regularly to find out how you're doing and encourage you to keep at it.

2. Share the five TRACE steps with your husband, and ask him to name one or two of your bad habits that inhibit the romance he feels toward you. If you start feeling defensive at his comments, refrain from speaking angrily, defending yourself, or pointing out his weaknesses to make yourself feel better. Instead, remind yourself that you need to know where to improve if you're going to become good at TRACE-ing a new path toward romance. Tell yourself that your husband already loves you the way you are, that you want to improve to please God and delight your husband, and that God will help you TRACE a new path. Write his response in your prayer journal as a reminder to focus on these particular areas.

CHAPTER SIX

Thinking Differently About Sex

And the two are united into one.
This is a great mystery.
—EPHESIANS 5:31–32

We need never be ashamed to talk about
what God was not ashamed to create.
—MARABEL MORGAN, *THE TOTAL WOMAN*

Let me begin by saying that this chapter will not address all the needs or hurts associated with sex. With all the implications for women today, sex is a topic you may need to explore further, and I encourage you to do just that. In the appendix, I've recommended several excellent resources that provide guidance to those who have been hurt by negative sexual experiences. If that describes you, I urge you to seek help from a professional therapist, check into the resources available in your church, or join an Open Hearts Ministry Journey Group (www.ohmin.org). Until you deal with your buried pain, it will affect you and your marriage in a multitude of ways difficult to comprehend.

Sex is huge. The impact it has in each of our lives, for good or bad, is enormous.

My sexual journey has been long and bumpy, and while I'm in a better place now than ever before, it's still a long way from where I desire to be. Tom and I became sexually active early in our relationship; we got pregnant before we were married. Memories of my honeymoon include bouts of morning sickness and irritation over my new husband's insatiable appetite for sex. It was a rough start. Sex soon became the lightning rod of our relationship.

Various sources cite sex as one of the top three issues couples argue about. In my discussions with women, young and old, the subject of sex invariably comes up. When I taught a neighborhood Bible study on marriage, sex generated the most discussion. As soon as they knew I was willing to discuss the subject, they asked one question after another. They wanted trustworthy answers to questions about issues such as dressing provocatively, dealing with pornography, and coping with never-ending exhaustion. They wanted to know what God says about sex in light of an ever-changing culture. It is my prayer that this chapter will provide a starting point for an honest dialogue among women about the profound mystery of sex.

CHANGE THE WAY YOU THINK

Christian women often have a difficult time gaining a clear understanding of how to think about sex, for we hear conflicting messages from the church, our culture, and other people who have influence in our lives. If you or your spouse wants more from your sexual relationship, you must change your thoughts. These new thoughts will spur new actions, and you'll begin to discover an amazing aspect of your marriage you might otherwise have missed.

What Does God Think About Sex?

Do you know what God's thoughts are about sex? If you knew, you might be surprised. Furthermore, if you replaced your thoughts with His, you would act differently. Paul instructed in Romans 12:2, "Don't copy the behavior and customs of this world, but let God transform you into a new person by changing the way you think. Then you will know what God wants you to do, and you will know how good and pleasing and perfect His will really is." Right thoughts precede right action.

God designed sex with six purposes in mind: creation of life, oneness, knowledge, pleasure, defense against temptation, and comfort.[1]

Creation of Life. "God blessed them and said to them, 'Be fruitful and increase in number; fill the earth and subdue it. Rule over the fish of the sea and the birds of the air and over every living creature that moves on the ground'" (Genesis 1:28 NIV). The purpose of creating life holds significant importance in God's eyes, however it is not something very many Christian couples take seriously.

Tom and I were thrilled to welcome three children into the world, but I wasn't particularly open to the possibility of having more. So we took matters into our own hands to restrict future births—a decision I regretted a few years later.

Projections by the Pew Research Center's Forum on Religion and Public Life indicate that over the next twenty years the world's Muslim population will grow twice as fast as the non-Muslim population. By 2030, Muslims will make up more than a quarter of the global population.[2] These are staggering statistics! Maybe we should take God's command to be fruitful and increase in number more seriously.

As a follower of Jesus Christ, I love Muslims and want them to come to a full knowledge of Him. But who will show them the way if the Christian population dwindles by comparison?

The command to be fruitful and multiply demands our attention! Pray that God will accomplish His purpose through your family and trust Him to guide you each step of the way.

Oneness. Genesis 2:24 says, "This explains why a man leaves his father and mother and is joined to his wife, and the two are united into one." The original Hebrew word translated *joined* means "to adhere" or "stick to" each other. Paula Rinehart explains, "The glue amazingly enough, is sex. . . . It's a frame that holds a husband and wife together when the days grow dark and no words are strong enough to make everything all right."[3] The act of sex forms a bond with your husband like nothing else can. Your sexual relationship with your husband holds you close through all the joys and struggles of your life. Your marriage is strengthened by the glue or frame that is sex.

In sex, we experience desire and pursuit that culminates in rapture. You feel complete with your husband. "For many people, sex is the most tangible experience they know of feeling loved and wanted by another person."[4] God uses that experience to help you comprehend a greater mystery. In reference to the "one flesh" sexual relationship between a husband and wife, the apostle Paul says, "This is a great mystery, but it is an illustration of the way Christ and the church are one" (Ephesians 5:32). Within the act of sex, God has hidden a truth so grand and mysterious it nearly defies comprehension. Rinehart explains:

> Christ uses His relationship with the bride—His church—to unlock the mystery of sex. At the heart of the mystery of sex is a God who pursues you to the end of the earth, not to pin you into submission, but to embrace you at the core of your being with a love beyond that of any man, a love that penetrates your deepest fears and heals your shame, a love that will not let you go. We are never truly free until our hearts are ravished in the love of God.[5]

Though your sexual experience may fall short of a masterpiece, it can provide glimpses into God's great desire for you.

Knowledge. Genesis 4:1 (NKJV) says, "Now Adam knew Eve his wife, and she conceived and bore Cain." God wants you to experience deeper levels of intimacy—an increased depth of "knowing"—that can only develop between you and your husband through sex. To know and be known beyond what you can experience with any other person is a deep reservoir of blessing for you to draw from. Realizing you are known and loved brings joy.

Pleasure. God thinks the pleasure you experience through sex is a good thing. In fact, He designed your bodies to find pleasure in sex. Proverbs 5:18–19 says, "Let your wife be a fountain of blessing for you. Rejoice in the wife of your youth. She is a loving doe, a graceful deer. Let her breasts satisfy you always. May you always be captivated by her love." The Amplified Bible translation of these verses says, "Let her be as the loving hind and pleasant doe (tender, gentle, attractive)— let her bosom satisfy you at all times, and always be transported with delight in her love." The King James Version says, "Be thou ravished always with her love." Breasts that satisfy, love that captivates, delight that transports, and love that ravishes—yeah, that's pleasure!

God has designed the sexual relationship to please you and your husband. Bind this knowledge to your own thinking, and let it motivate you to give and seek until you find pleasure.

Protection from Temptation. In 1 Corinthians, Paul writes, "The husband should not deprive his wife of sexual intimacy, which is her right as a married woman, nor should the wife deprive her husband. The wife gives authority over her body to her husband, and the husband also gives authority over his body to his wife" (7:3–4). If you've been married for any length of time, you already know this can be a tall order for most women. But understanding the reasons behind these instructions can help motivate us to change our thinking and begin to fulfill this part of God's Word. The surrounding context of the passage presents the reasoning:

> But because there is so much sexual immorality, each man should have his own wife, and each woman should have her own husband. . . . So do not deprive each other of sexual relations. The only exception to this rule would be the agreement of both husband and wife to refrain from sexual intimacy for a limited time, so they can give themselves more completely to prayer. Afterward they should come together again so that Satan won't be able to tempt them because of their lack of self-control. (7:2, 5)

111

Because we live in a highly sexualized culture, sex within marriage safeguards us against temptation. Depriving each other of sex (aside from health reasons, or the exception the Bible mentions) may lower your self-control, and the lack of self-control leads to dangerous waters. The bond formed and maintained through sex helps you and your husband resist outside forces aimed against your marriage. Are your thoughts in line with God's in this area?

Comfort. God desires you to experience comfort from the stresses and sorrows of life through sex. David comforted Bathsheba after the death of their child by laying with her (2 Samuel 12:24). Rebekah comforted Isaac after the death of his mother in the same way (Genesis 24:67). You too can find comfort in sex.

This is a relatively new thought for me, but I've found it to be true. Often, during stressful, difficult times, my sexual desire seems lessened. But the realization that God designed sex as a means of experiencing comfort has changed the way I think—and my actions have changed too. Now I'm motivated to embrace and extend this gift of comfort when life is difficult. I've changed my thinking to match God's on this point, and it's had a positive effect on our sex life.

These are God's thoughts about sex, which is His gift for you to experience within the bonds of marriage. Regardless of what the world, the church, or others have said, it's time to align your thoughts with God's. When you think like God thinks concerning His creation of sex, you are on the best possible path to His good, pleasing, and perfect plan for your sex life.

WHAT DOES YOUR HUSBAND THINK ABOUT SEX?

You may have strong opinions about what your husband thinks about sex, but are your ideas accurate? Until you can get inside your husband's mind and look through his eyes, it's difficult to know for sure. Fortunately for us, in her excellent book, *For Women Only: What You Need to Know about the Inner Lives of Men,* author Shaunti Feldhahn dug deep into men's minds. She interviewed and surveyed hundreds of men. Her objective was to discover what women need to know about men on a variety of subjects. Concerning the subject of sex she says, "On each survey and in my random interviews around the country, an urgent theme emerged: Men want more sex than they are getting. And what's more, they believe that the women who love them don't seem to realize that this is a crisis—not only for the man, but for the relationship."[6]

Okay, maybe you're not surprised to hear about the strength of your husband's desire for sex, but there's a deeper desire he has which he may not have been able to (or felt the freedom to) communicate with you. Until you understand why sex is so important to him— emotionally—you won't understand why this is a crisis for men.

His Thoughts About His Desire

According to Shaunti, "97 percent of men said 'getting enough sex' wasn't, by itself, enough—they wanted to feel wanted. . . . The survey showed that *even if they were getting all the sex they wanted,* three out of four men would still feel empty if their wife wasn't both engaged and satisfied."[7]

Your husband isn't interested solely in the physical benefits of sex! His need is deeply emotional. He needs you to need him. His unspoken hope is that you desire him as much as he desires you. It's not enough for you to "let" him meet his physical needs with your body; he longs to connect with you at a deeper emotional level.

If you think that your husband's need for sex is strictly a matter of the physical, you could argue that your physical need for sleep, for instance, should count equally. Understanding that sex means far more than just meeting the physical needs of your husband changes everything. This should help you to relate more closely with him. You, too, have emotional needs you want your husband to meet. You both long to feel loved, desired, and confident in your relationship. When you purposefully and lovingly attend to your husband sexually, you fulfill deep longings in his heart. His response of gratitude may surprise you. A sexually satisfied husband is likely to move mountains on behalf of the wife who fulfills him.

At this point, you might be fearfully wondering just what is required of a "fully engaged" wife. Shaunti asked husbands this question. "All that means, [husbands] say, is a wife who makes the first move once in a while and who brings all of her attentions and passion for her man to bed with her."[8] That's all it takes!

The men Shaunti surveyed admitted that when their sexual needs were unmet, they felt wounded. One man said, "If she doesn't want to, I feel incredible rejection."[9] Shaunti summarizes very clearly: "Your lack of desire can send him into depression."[10]

Most writers I've read on the subject of sex compare your husband's emotional need for sex with your emotional need for communication. If your husband were to stop talking to you for a week, how would you feel? Rejected? Depressed? This is comparable to how your husband feels when you dismiss his sexual needs entirely, or allow him to use your body while your mind and emotions are far away. Inwardly, your husband interprets your behavior as rejection. On Shaunti's survey, one man stated, "'No' is not no to sex—as she might feel. It is no to me as I am."[11] Every fiber in my being responds to this heart-cry!

It's easy to see how prolonged rejection could lead toward depression. The oneness, emotional intimacy, and protection your husband experiences from a healthy sexual relationship with you insulate him from all the other rejections he encounters on a daily basis. You are the one person he can't endure to be rejected by.

As you meet your husband's emotional need for sex by engaging with your body as well as your mind, he will reap all the blessings God gives through the sexual union—children, oneness, pleasure, comfort, knowledge, and protection. In addition, he will experience two specific benefits. First, sex will make him feel loved and desired.

Secondly, it will give him confidence.[12] Helping your husband feel more loved, desired, and confident can't help but bless you too.

His Lack of Desire and/or Unusual Sexual Behavior

While the stereotypical husband is interested in sex at least twice as much as his wife, many women have painful stories of a husband who lacks desire for sexual intimacy or exhibits unusual behavior during intimate moments. Please know, you are not alone, and help is available.

According to Boston Medical Group, there are several factors that could result in a loss of libido in men. *Physical factors* include being over- or under-weight, which can affect a man's hormonal levels and leave him feeling less sexual, and aging. *Psychological factors* that lessen or inhibit a man's desire for sex include depression, fatigue, trauma, performance anxiety, and body image concerns. *Medical conditions* may of course play a role, and it is worth checking on the side effects of any prescription medications that your husband is taking.[13]

If your husband exhibits unusual or sinful behavior such as inexplicably or violently pushing away your sexual advances or looking at pornography, particularly of men, it may indicate he's suffered sexual abuse as a child. If you suspect this is true, Cecil Murphey's book, *When a Man You Love Was Abused*, will help you know how to respond. If your husband has been sexually abused, chances are high that it's affecting your sex life. Remember that nothing is too difficult for God (Jeremiah 32:17), and turn to Him for wisdom and strength to deal with your husband's sexual wounds.

Before approaching your husband on these sensitive issues, approach God in prayer. Ask Him for the wisdom you need to speak the truth in love. Do some additional reading as God prompts. Read chapter 11 of *Intimate Issues*, "What Do I Do When HE Has a Headache?" Or read Cecil Murphey's book. It will also be helpful to read chapter 8 in *The Beautiful Wife*, "Speaking Truth in Love" before talking to your husband. Respect his need for privacy and share your concerns only with a trusted mentor, pastor, or counselor.

God bless you on this journey.

His Thoughts About Your Body

Because your husband is visual, he wants to see you naked—yes, you with the cellulite and stretch marks. Do you think having a figure like Barbie would be ideal? Think again. If Barbie was a real woman, she'd have to walk on all fours due to her proportions! Barbie doesn't have a figure that works for real women. Yet it's easy to be inhibited in the bedroom if you believe your body doesn't stack up against the images our culture promotes as sexy. It's hard to miss the discrepancies between our own bodies and those women we see on billboards, television, and in magazine ads. Our cellulite, stretch marks, and sagging body parts mock us among the chorus of airbrushed, photoshopped, augmented perfection.

If you're allowing culture's influence to keep you from proudly using your beautiful feminine body to seduce your husband, it's time to change the way you think. Your body, and the way in which you care for it, is important to your husband—but not in the way you might think.

> It's not about being tiny. If she doesn't take care of herself, dresses sloppily around me all the time, never exercises, and has no energy to go out and do things together, I feel like she's choosing not to do something that she should know is important to me. And then it becomes a real issue because it affects her ability to do things and her *self-worth and desire*—and then it affects me.[14]

Your husband isn't as interested in your body's perfection as he is that you confidently move your body in his direction. Laura Schlessinger concurs:

> The men who wrote to me commenting on this issue surprisingly were in agreement that there was no absolute rating system in their minds about perfect female bodies when it came to their wives. Most of the men were describing their desire for their wives to dress (and undress) and behave somewhat coquettishly.

Their sense of well-being was very tied into their wives indulging them with visual input and seductive behavior.[15]

How should a real woman think about her body and its power to seduce her husband? Consider Carolyn, a wife soon to be sixty:

As I age, the old body deteriorates. I've got stretch marks from three babies, cellulite, and varicose veins. My breasts sag, wrinkles abound, but as my body has fallen, my expertise as a lover has risen. I really think my dear husband of forty years still sees my body as it was when I was young because he receives such pleasure from it.[16]

Carolyn's wise thinking has led her to wise actions. Using her body to bring pleasure and delight to her husband has kept him a happy man—in spite of any imperfections from her point of view. "It's better to be sensuous than to have a perfect '10' body."[17]

WHAT DO YOU THINK ABOUT SEX?

Knowing God's and your husband's thoughts on sex is a good beginning, but our present concerns and past hurts can hinder us from enjoying the blessings of sex. Where can you go with all of your thoughts? Bring them to God—ask Him for help.

Your Thoughts About Its Importance

In her book, *The Power of a Praying Wife*, author Stormie Omartian writes, "After twenty years of praying with women about their failing, struggling, unfulfilling, or dead marriages, I've observed that frequently the sexual relationship is a low priority in their minds. It isn't that the wife cares nothing about that part of her life. It's that there are so many other things screaming for her attention, such as raising children, work, finances, managing a home, emotional stress, exhaustion, sickness, and marital strife."[18]

How do you drum up the will for sex when you're thinking about the lunches you need to make before school tomorrow morning? For many of us, it's a giant leap to go from peanut butter sandwiches to sex. Making this leap requires us to change our thinking.

Also, there may be times when negative thoughts about your husband keep you from getting in the mood. You may feel angry or unsupported by your husband. It's tempting to refuse him sexually during these times. This was a habit I formed during the first twelve years of our marriage. When I was angry with Tom, I withheld sex. It's a dangerous habit, and it doesn't reward you with the intimacy and understanding you're looking for. Changing the way you think about getting your needs met may help reverse this negative cycle where no one wins.

Stormie Omartian continues: "A husband . . . has trouble hearing anything his wife says or seeing what she needs when that area of his being [sex] is neglected. Wives sometimes have it backwards. They think, *We can have sex after we get these other issues settled.* But actually there is a far greater chance of settling the other issues if sex comes first."[19] This makes sense if you consider how your husband thinks about sex. If your husband feels rejected by your lack of sexual response to him, he may have trouble hearing what you say or seeing what you need. Rejection is a powerful emotion. If you're experiencing a disconnect or miscommunication with your husband, try working the issue out after sex, not before.

You have the power to dismantle barriers between you and your husband by entering (dare I say?) *joyfully* into sexual union with him, even in light of your unmet needs. You'll have to ask God for help on this one—but He will be there to help you!

Your Thoughts About Past Hurts

If your thoughts concerning sex are marked by the pain of abortion, past negative sexual experiences, abuse, or pornography, you are not alone. Many suffer from past sexual sins or wounds. But there is good news. I know from my own as well as others' experiences that you can know freedom, healing, and hope regardless of past hurts.

Because sexual sin produces shame, it's difficult for many women to be honest about their sexual experiences. I should know. Until recently, I was ashamed to admit that I was pregnant before marriage and sexually abused as a child. Often, it is still difficult to admit.

Shameful sexual memories are easier to bury in the deep places of your heart than to expose to the light of truth. But, although you may have buried them, they're not dead. Burying shame doesn't stop it from causing you great pain or affecting your marriage. It must be exposed to the light of God's love and healing power. Though not an easy process, it's important to take the first steps now! Don't let sexual shame rob you of more life than it already has. I encourage you to seek the help you need to receive healing. Talk to a Christian counselor or trustworthy friend, read the book *Intimate Issues* which gives practical advice on many sexual issues, or join a Christian support group dedicated to the issues you face.

Maybe you don't carry the weight of sexual baggage but you're still confused about sex with so many voices shaping your thinking. Most likely the loudest voice you hear is that of modern culture. Women are adversely affected by the cultural messages bombarding us. You can't always cover your ears or make it go away, but you can encourage yourself and your friends by speaking the counter-cultural message of God's truth on a regular basis. This message helps you think differently, and consequently act differently. When your actions change, you'll experience better results sexually than ever before.

Whatever your story, God loves you and wants you to enjoy a satisfying sexual relationship with your husband. He longs to heal you from the pain of past sexual experiences so you can enjoy true freedom. He may even be calling you to share your path to freedom with others, so they, too, can be free.

IMPROVING YOUR SEX LIFE

When we change our thinking about sex, we can change the way we act. These actions will lead us to a sex life that is good and pleasing— to us as well as to God.

Prioritizing Commitments

Dr. Kevin Leman cautions: "When we live life at the pace of a NASCAR race, sex is one of the first things that goes."[20] I'm sure you can relate to this statement, as I can. One of the greatest deterrents keeping us from a healthy sex life is exhaustion. Women are exhausted keeping up with our often self-imposed schedules. I'm not referring to the work that helps make ends meet, but rather all those extra activities we cram into every spare hour of the week. Dr. Leman specifically advises couples to change their weekly schedules for the benefit of their sex life. "I'd say if you're gone more than two evenings a week, something needs to give."[21]

Something needs to give? Many of you may be in shock right now. You can't begin to envision what you would cut from your busy schedule. With church involvement, your children's school and extracurricular activities, as well as other interests, you're lucky if you're *home* together two nights a week—not the other way around!

The busyness will never end unless you end it. Even as empty-nesters, Tom and I have to protect our schedules in order to have more than one or two nights home alone.

Do you need motivation to begin eliminating activities? Think of it this way. If more time equals better sex which equals a better marriage and happier children, then what's the point of all the busyness? What value does your busy schedule give to your life, your marriage, and your children? Is it adding to or taking away from your happiness and sense of well-being?

I suggest that you sit down with your husband and analyze your schedules. If you were to eliminate all but two nights' activities, what would you purge? Whacking away at your schedule may not be easy physically or emotionally.

Physically speaking, Tom and I have learned that adrenaline floods our body in order to keep up with the demands of a hectic pace. The more adrenaline your body produces, the more it craves. When you begin slowing down, your body will miss the continuous flow of adrenaline, and you'll feel out of sorts for a while.[22] But over time, you will adjust to living with less adrenaline and will feel healthier and happier.

Emotionally, it's hard to say no to wonderful programs or requests for help at church, kids' activities, and other things clamoring for your participation. You may think that if you don't fill that position at church, no one will or people will think poorly of you. You may be convinced that your child may be the next basketball, soccer, or ballet star with the right training. Or perhaps you feel that one more class may help you land the job of your dreams.

Our culture echoes these messages loudly.

The best way to determine what God is saying about your schedule is to ask Him. He'll let you know. Psalm 91:15 says, "When they call on me, I will answer." It's such a simple act of trust, calling out to God, believing He'll show you the way. Listen to His voice, as opposed to the culture's or your own. God will breathe new life into the lungs of your marriage and sex life when you remove the weight of overcommitment.

Getting in the Mood

Life is busy, I know. It's difficult to get in the mood and have compassion toward your husband and his sexual needs—physical and emotional—when you have so many other things on your mind. "If desire is more psychological than physical, it's not difficult to understand why stress would result in the body's sexual boycott."[23] Keeping in mind the blessings sex offers (creation of life, oneness, pleasure, knowledge, protection, and comfort) as well as how the lack of sex affects husbands (physically and emotionally) should provide some of the power and motivation we need to focus on getting in the mood—flipping the switch.

In addition, I've found compartmentalizing my thoughts—categorizing and storing them accordingly—allows more brain matter allotted to thoughts of sex. If you have to unload some data from your brain, make notes of things to be done the following day. Ask other women how they clear crowded thoughts from their brain to make room for thoughts of sex.

Maybe aromatherapy helps you. If you haven't tried it, you may not understand, but just a whiff of a beautiful scent has the power to change your emotional disposition. If you're tired and sweaty, take a bath and spritz some perfume. Turn on some music. Eat some chocolate. Experiment to identify what it takes to flip the switch in your brain.

Seducing Your Husband

Your husband wants you to seduce him. Have you ever thought about *how* to be seductive? If you've rarely thought about this question, begin reading the Song of Solomon for starters. Check out resources such as *Simply Romantic Nights* by FamilyLife. Ask God to enliven your imagination as to how you can introduce the element of seduction into your lovemaking. Your seductive behavior will have a great effect on your husband.

Seduce Using Visuals. Dress for success! Remember that Bible study discussion on sex I told you about? One woman struggling with her sexual relationship sheepishly asked me if I thought it was wrong that she wore tattered sweatpants to bed each night. Yes, it's wrong! Not only does this type of attire do nothing for arousing your husband, it does nothing for getting you in the mood. It also signals to your husband that you're not interested—which most men take as rejection.

Find out what your husband likes. I was surprised to discover that Tom doesn't always like all that fancy lingerie. Form fitting tank-tops and little panties can be alluring yet comfortable. When I do wear lingerie, I find it's never on more than a few minutes! It really does the trick. Afterward, slip into something more comfortable—but try to avoid old, holey sweatpants if at all possible.

Seduce Using Touch. I've heard many men admit that one of their primary love languages is physical touch. My husband and sons feel most loved when they are touched. So use the power of touch to seduce your husband.

Kiss his forehead, neck, and chest. Run your fingers through his hair and over the back of his head. Place your hand on his leg, give it a squeeze, and let your hand linger there. Rub his arms. Place your hand over the back of his hand, entwine your fingers and squeeze. (Tips courtesy of Tom!)

Offer to give your husband a hot-oil back massage, or ask if he'll give you one. If he knows ahead of time what will follow, he might be eager. Begin thinking like a seductive woman and release your inner-sexy for your husband.

Seduce Using Scent. Aromatherapy is capable of transporting your sexual intimacy from the mundane to the sublime. Before you laugh and write me off, consider how you feel when entering a home where a delectable meal has been prepared and the aroma is wafting throughout the house as you enter. The scent signals your brain that a wonderful meal is coming! Since foreplay often begins in a woman's brain, jump-start your sexual intimacy with a good dose of aromatherapy.

When Tom wears my favorite cologne, it's a turn-on! I just want to bury my head in his neck. Taking the time and effort to spritz on a bit of perfume or mist the sheets with a fragrant linen spray before bed are special touches that get noticed.

Go to your favorite bath and body shop with your husband and do a "sniff" test to select your favorite perfumes, oils, and lotions. If your husband knows their intended purpose, he'll probably be more than willing to visit the mall with you.

Seduce Using Music. Let's face it, music is a powerful medium, capable of evoking a particular mood with lightning speed. Why not employ a force this powerful in your sex life?

What music puts you in the mood? Play your favorite tunes whether it's Pavorotti, Sting, or Music of the African Rainforest. Turn it on and let it turn you on.

All this work to change your thinking about sex, prioritize your commitments, get in the mood, and seduce your husband is not just for your husband's benefit. Having a fulfilling sexual relationship with your husband is one of the best ways to feel confident and beautiful. One woman shared with me that before she was married, she had insecurities because of her not-so-bountiful bosom. Now, because of a fulfilling sex life with her husband, she has more confidence in her appearance than ever before.

Think counterculturally and begin using your body to give your husband pleasure. You will reap the rewards of feeling better about yourself and enjoying greater intimacy and emotional connection with your husband. I pray your sex life will be blessed!

Reflection

1. Knowing the benefits God has provided through sex, how will this change of thinking affect your actions?
2. Which of Shaunti Feldhahn's survey results impacted you the most? Why? Does this information motivate you to change your actions? How do you think this change of action will affect your sex life? Your marriage?
3. What is the biggest deterrent to your sex life? Journal your thoughts.
4. What specific steps could you take to reclaim the benefits of sex in your marriage?
5. What fears, if any, do you have regarding sex?

First Steps

1. Reread the section, "What Does Your Husband Think About Sex?" to determine any areas that require a change in your thinking. Journal your response.

2. Open the lines of communication with your husband about your sexual relationship. Allow him the opportunity to share his feelings; carefully listen to all he says. Share your feelings and fears. Journal a response.

3. Devise a plan with changes you can make (based on your husband's input above)—with God's and possibly other people's help—to recapture a vital sex life. Record the plan in your journal.

CHAPTER SEVEN

Opening Lines of Communication

*There is a time for everything . . . a time to be quiet
and a time to speak up.*
—ECCLESIASTES 3:1, 7

*We have two ears and one mouth so that we can listen
twice as much as we speak.*
—EPICTETUS

A few years back, Tom and I had a whopper of a communication breakdown.

We were driving home from my parent's house when my husband spotted the convertible of his dreams—a 1952 MGB replica. Tom had long admired this car, dreaming of the day he would own one—even keeping a toy version on his desk to remind him of his desire. Now, his dream car was there before his eyes sitting beside the road with a "For Sale" sign taped to the windshield. Twenty-four hours later, we owned it.

We drove that car for hours on end. Tom loves hot summer days. For him, there is no better way to enjoy life than riding in a convertible. I enjoyed it too, because it meant I got large amounts of quality time with my husband. We savored many conversations in that convertible. Over several years, we logged many thousands of miles, exploring the back roads of Michigan, Indiana, and Wisconsin.

Riding in the convertible was great fun—until my back started to give me serious problems. My neck became increasingly stiff while bracing against the summer winds, and when I stepped out of the convertible my hips would ache. It was clear I had a problem. I began visiting the chiropractor on a regular basis—something I had never done.

I wish I could say I used good communication skills to share my problem with my husband, but I didn't. As a result, Tom and I experienced hurt, confusion, and loneliness. We were cut off from all the benefits that good communication offers.

Although the advice in this chapter is fitted to a major disagreement in the life of your marriage, several of the tips mentioned are applicable for everyday use. Using them will improve the quality of communication you enjoy with your husband.

Good communication starts with being direct and kind, as well as choosing the proper time and place. To effect real change in your marriage or simply to get an improved understanding of what's really being said, you must also practice listening and have intentional dialogue with your husband in order to open the lines of communication.

BE DIRECT

Have you ever noticed that your husband doesn't pick up on your subtle hints? I was once sent an email entitled "Guys' Rules" that explains this fact:

Ask for what you want.
Let us be clear on this one:
Subtle hints do not work!
Strong hints do not work!
Obvious hints do not work!
Just say it!

I knew that riding in Tom's dream car was the cause of my physical pain for a full year before I spoke directly about it. Instead of coming right out and telling Tom that the car was the cause of my pain, I dropped hints and innuendoes, like:

"The strong winds are really beating on my head today."
"Do you ever notice how the whole car shakes when we go over a bump?"
"I don't think my neck would tighten up so at night if we had a heater in the car."
"It's hot today . . . Don't you wish this car had an air conditioner and we could put the roof up?"
"How do you feel about other convertibles?"

On and on it went. For a whole year, I hinted at what I wanted to say—that the car hurt my back, neck, and hips. So, Tom tried to fix the car's shaking by installing new shocks. He added a headrest for me to lean my head on and replaced the old foam in the seats with new foam. He tried to put out all the little fires I'd started with hints, but it was too late. The damage was already done. None of Tom's improvements changed my pain. Still, I didn't directly reveal my true feelings. I obviously wasn't following the "Guys' Rules" for communication.

Because I was indirect, Tom had to connect the dots of my hinted messages himself, and the dots formed a false message. He thought I was trying to tell him that I wanted a new, more prestigious car. He reacted to this stubbornly. In turn, his stubbornness caused me to feel he valued his car more than me and my health. We experienced a classic communication breakdown because I was afraid to be honest and direct. Yes, afraid!

Why was I afraid to be direct?

Satan instigates fear whenever he can. Fear keeps us from communicating directly, thereby withholding the very intimacy with our husbands that we crave. I was afraid Tom would be disappointed that his dream car was the source of my neck and back pain. I was also afraid that he might continue driving it without me. I'd be left home alone, but if he gave up the car to stay home with me, I'd be the cause of his disappointment. I didn't want either of those solutions, so I avoided direct communication.

The result was hurt feelings on both sides. I felt hurt that Tom wasn't picking up on my hints that were meant to lead him to conclude that we needed a different convertible. I was lonely and waiting for him to rescue me from my pain. Tom was hurt and confused—why weren't all his efforts to fix the problems I'd hinted at satisfying me?

If I could do it all over again, I would be direct: "This car has been a blessing, but now, it hurts my neck, back, and hips. I like our convertible driving, and I don't want to quit. Maybe a different convertible would work better, one with better suspension, comfortable seats, and special protection from the wind. This is a great disappointment to me, and I know it's disappointing for you, honey, and I'm sorry for that."

What a different picture direct communication paints! Had I been direct, we would have been able to work on finding an effective solution together.

BE KIND

Directness is one key to effective communication. So is kindness. A friend of mine once remarked, "How different the world would be if we were kind to one another." This simple concept is difficult to consistently live out. In the matter of the convertible, I failed on a number of levels to be kind, which strained our ability to communicate.

Do you know anyone with a direct communication approach void of kindness? Often, these people are described as "tactless." One such man lived across the street from me when I was a young mom. He was gruff, and he spoke his mind, his words void of kindness. Before I could receive anything from him, God had to reveal to me that his heart was good and he wasn't purposefully being unkind. I'm sure you know people like this, but you can choose a better way by being direct *and* kind.

By the time I blurted out directly the real reason I was unhappy with the convertible, my communication was void of kindness: "I'm not riding in that car one more minute because it's hurting my back!" Tom's reaction wasn't what I'd hoped for. My harsh words closed all lines of communication.

I wish I'd said far gentler words. I would have mentioned the many good times we had enjoyed in the convertible and that I'd love to continue our driving adventures. I also would have expressed my disappointment for the loss we'd both feel. Had I applied kindness, Tom would have realized I cared about him, valued the memories we'd made, and desired to continue this activity we both enjoyed. I would have opened the lines of communication and we could have moved toward a solution together.

CHOOSE THE PROPER TIME AND PLACE

It is also critical to consider the proper time and place to speak. When I did finally tell Tom that I was no longer willing to ride in the convertible, I chose the worst possible time!

For the past several months, he had been planning a weekend driving trip with some close friends of ours who also owned convertibles. He had explored the route months earlier, made reservations at a bed and breakfast, highlighted the attractions on a map, and created a PowerPoint presentation to whet everyone's appetite. All that remained to be done was to have a predeparture party with our friends, pack our bags, and put gas in the car.

When I finally made the leap to communicate about my back pain with my husband, it was the week prior to our departure. I'm wincing right along with you as I recall my words once more: *"I'm not riding in that car one more minute because it's hurting my back!"*

Needless to say, this was not the proper time to communicate my need and dig in my heels! I had procrastinated for a full year, and *now*

I wasn't going to budge? One more trip wouldn't have been my undo-ing—it would have caused me discomfort, but I could have easily waited until after the trip to talk with Tom about my problem.

After I dropped my ultimatum on him, there was an icy silence between us, so I was unaware that he was still planning on taking the trip whether I went or not. Continuing with his original plans, he invited our convertible buddies over for his presentation of the trip, during which I sulked in the corner waiting for the right opportunity to announce to our friends that I wouldn't be going. In the end, Tom went on the trip alone. Our friends, who didn't want to take sides, made other plans. I stayed home and cried. What should have been discussed privately a year earlier suddenly became public, causing needless pain for Tom, our friends, and me.

There are other places you may want to avoid when discussing sensitive issues. Talking over issues in bed can be counterproductive to a fulfilling sex life (and could violate the biblical principle of not letting the sun go down on your anger), although it may be one of the only places you share alone. Enjoy your bedroom as a sanctuary and respite, and raise potential controversy there only when necessary to avoid sensitive discussions in front of children.

Tom and I now enjoy discussing issues at our local coffee shop. Focused on a specific point of discussion while sharing a delicious cup of coffee, we're committed to working through the issue at hand. Often, we need more time, so we put the conversation on hold until another date, which we set before leaving. Meeting publicly also helps avoid escalation.

Choosing the wrong time and place to communicate can leave you hurt, lonely, and isolated. Make the effort to communicate directly and kindly on a regular basis. Deal with issues as they arise; this eliminates the need for dynamite. You're not doing yourself any favors by procrastinating when there is a need to communicate.

In my particular situation, proper timing meant speaking sooner. But sometimes, proper timing dictates that we *wait* to speak to our husbands. Ecclesiastes 3:1, 7 says, "There is a time for everything . . . a time to be quiet and a time to speak."

Choosing the proper time and place opens the lines of effective communication.

LISTEN

God knows how difficult it is for us to listen, and He reminds us of its importance again and again throughout the Bible. James 1:19 says, "My dear brothers and sisters, be quick to listen, slow to speak, and slow to get angry." Isaiah 55:3 says, "Come to me with your ears wide open. Listen, for the life of your soul is at stake."

Do you listen twice as much as you speak? Listening more and speaking less is challenging. Consider that "we all make many mistakes, but those who control their tongues can also control ourselves in every other way" (James 3:2). Desiring to increase self-control, I've recently taken on the challenge of controlling my tongue. Yet even when I am focused on talking less, I find myself falling far short of my goal.

After the public convertible-driving showdown, Tom and I began the long, sometimes painful, process of listening to one another. Since we had both sustained much hurt, it was difficult for each of us to listen without defending ourselves—but we slowly made progress.

When I stopped talking, I learned that because Tom had put so much time, energy, and care into his dream car, he didn't want to give it up—he wanted to continue driving it. Thinking of Tom riding without me was painful. Thoughts of loneliness and abandonment tempted me to let him have an earful, but I eventually let him get all his thoughts out.

Tom listened, too. Through my direct and kind communication, he learned that I was concerned enough about my health that I wasn't going to ride in the MGB anymore—even though it was something I valued. Overcoming past, faulty assumptions made it difficult for him to trust my message, but he listened nevertheless.

It can be difficult to reverse the trend to interrupt or to defend yourself, but you'll feel so much better when you listen with an open mind. Like me, you'll find you can learn a lot, and live to tell about it!

Listening is so difficult for me that I actually have to tell myself to stop talking. Such self-talk does wonders for me; it encourages me to be still and listen. I often tell myself, "I can listen to this and live through it without saying a word—there's nothing to be afraid of."

Why is it difficult for so many of us to control our tongues? It's most difficult for me to listen when I disagree with Tom. I have an urge to defend myself or correct his thinking. This represents a not-so-subtle mix of fear and pride. When fear and pride control our tongues, our words close the lines of communication in our marriage. Satan infiltrates our thoughts with lies meant to produce fear, so it is critical that we combat this invasion by using the sword (words) of truth.

Listen Actively

When you listen, you might try the childhood game of locking your lips and throwing away the key. Use body language to send the message that you're listening: face your husband, stand still (yes, this means you need to stop what you're doing), and fix your eyes on him with undivided attention. Do not think about what you are going to say or do next. Do not interrupt. Focus on what he says. When he is finished, respond in an "I'm interested in what you're saying" tone. Ask questions or repeat back key phrases; this lets him know that you are listening.

Listen to Understand

The purpose of listening is to understand your husband—to really "hear" what he's conveying. This is a skill worthy of praise in a wife. Proverbs 19:14 says, "Only the Lord can give an understanding wife."

God-given understanding enables you to unpack the message behind your husband's words. Your husband may be using words which, on the surface, have one meaning, but God-given understanding will reveal a deeper meaning. I'm not suggesting you use your own interpretive skills when listening to your husband—we've all heard stories about women who interpret their husband's words to their own advantage. Instead, I encourage you to grow in your ability to discern and understand what motivates his words.

When my friend's husband kept talking about quitting his job, she responded with panic and other negative emotions, which started a downward spiral of anger and hurt for both of them. When she realized she had not listened to understand, she discovered that he was trying to express how overwhelmed he was about a stressful work project. He didn't really want to quit, he just needed her to listen and provide encouragement.

INITIATE INTENTIONAL DIALOGUE

Do you find yourself wishing you had a husband with whom you could practice your listening skills? Many wives complain their husbands have difficulty sharing their true feelings. This is a grief to a wife who longs to experience the intimacy that good communication in marriage provides. If this is the case in your marriage, ask God to show you ways you may have contributed to your husband's silence. Listen to what God says, and repent for anything He reveals. Ask your husband for forgiveness and declare a renewed pledge to listen twice as much as you speak.

During a Focus on the Family broadcast, Pam Farrel, coauthor of *Men Are Like Waffles—Women Are Like Spaghetti,* told of a woman who was afraid to get married because she thought her fiancé, a race car driver, was "emotionally shallow."

> I said, "Go into the garage and repeat back key phrases and keep him talking." She says, "Okay." So she goes into the garage, and he's torqueing this and tweaking that and talking about rods and pistons. She is just repeating back all these car parts—she

doesn't even know what she's talking about—but she's duti-fully repeating back things, and he's working on the engine. He comes out from underneath that car, puts his hand on the hood, looks at her, and says, "Nobody has ever cared about my world like this. Nobody has ever loved me like this. Nobody's ever taken the time to understand my world like this. I am so excited to get married to you. I want to build you a big three-bedroom, two-bath home. Someday we'll have kids and I'll put up a swing set. I want to hang a swing on the front porch, and we'll sit there and drink lemonade and watch the sunset every night. I'm just so excited to get married to you." She told me later, "I never wanted to leave the garage again."[1]

Look for opportunities to have intentional dialogue and practice your listening skills. Your husband will be glad you did.

Imago Dialogue is one effective form of intentional dialogue you can use to open lines of communication with your husband.[2] It will help you to see from his perspective.

The goal is to provide your husband with a safe environment to say everything he needs to say. In the process, *both* of you will hear things you haven't heard before. There are three simple, but not always easy, steps to Imago Dialogue: mirroring, validation, and empathy.

Mirroring

Once your husband has communicated something to you, mirror back or repeat what you heard him say—using his words exactly, not your interpretation of his words. Begin with: "So you're saying . . . ?"

When he indicates that you correctly mirrored what he said, ask, "Is there more?" When he has finished a subject or thought, say, "Let me see if I have it all . . ." and repeat a summary—not an interpreta-tion—of what he has said so far.

There have been many occasions when I've correctly mirrored Tom's words, and this provided him the opportunity to "hear" what he actually said. If he "hears" a thought that doesn't accurately reflect his feelings, he tries again. He begins to see an image that his dialogue portrays when looking in the mirror of his words. This helps improve his communication and my listening skills.

There have been more occasions when I've interpreted his words rather than mirroring them—indicating my listening skills need improvement. It's necessary to block out all other thoughts, focusing on the words spoken in order to effectively reflect them.

When I worked to mirror Tom's words concerning the convertible, I had to block many fears from my mind. It took several attempts before I was successful, but eventually I accurately reflected his words: the MGB was his dream car. He didn't want to sell it just because I was no longer able to ride in it. He had worked hard to get it in terrific condition and had increased its value tremendously. This was an investment that he wanted to hang onto. He would continue to drive it.

Validation

After you've successfully mirrored your husband's words, the next step is validation. Validation doesn't require you to agree with what he is saying. You don't have to like it, either. It's not about who's right or who's wrong. The objective of validation is to confirm what your husband said and begin to see the issue from *his* perspective.

Validate your husband's words by saying, "That makes sense because . . ." If something doesn't make sense, you can say, "Can you help me understand?" After he responds with a clarification, go back to mirroring—"So you're saying . . ."—until you can see the situation from where he's standing and can validate how he could see it that way.

In regards to the convertible, validation was difficult because I disagreed with him. I felt it was pointless to keep a vehicle we couldn't both ride in. But seeing the situation from his perspective, it made sense that the MGB was important to Tom. He had dreamed of owning this car for nearly two decades. He'd spent hours reconditioning the car, upgrading even the smallest of details. I began to see from his perspective why he wanted to continue driving it.

Empathy

Once you've validated your husband's perspective, move on to the last step: empathy. Empathy is letting go of your own viewpoint for a few moments, seeing the issue from his angle, and feeling what he feels. You'll have to understand his perspective well in order to get this step right, but it's worth it.

Empathy says, "I can imagine you feel . . ." If you miss the mark, ask: "So then, what were you feeling?" and go back to mirroring.

I had to temporarily let go of my viewpoint that it made no sense to keep a car that didn't promote togetherness, in order to imagine how Tom must feel about giving up something so important to him. When I thought about how I would feel if asked to give up something important to me that I'd worked so hard on, I realized how Tom must feel. I could empathize with his feelings.

When you empathize with your husband, it will have the same effect on him as it would on you. He'll feel understood, and that will make him feel cared for. Walls will begin to melt. Intimacy will begin to grow.

Have you ever experienced the joy of being truly understood? If so, you can imagine how your husband will feel when you listen intentionally to him. If possible, practice Imago Dialogue in a Beautiful Womanhood small group or with other women. Then practice it on your husband. He'll be glad you did.

Tom drove the convertible all that autumn. It was important for me to keep busy at home when he was off driving. When he returned, I'd ask him about the drive and share his excitement for all he'd seen and experienced.

In January, Tom made his yearly trip to the auto show with our sons and some friends. Unbeknownst to me, he planned to investigate convertibles that included the protection I needed for my back. He found one—and it's a beauty. We picked up our Mini-Cooper convertible the following April and have logged thousands of miles on the back roads of Michigan, Wisconsin, and Minnesota ever since. We've savored many good times and great conversations.

Even though we're back on the road again, the memory of our communication breakdown still causes twinges of emotional pain, so we continue to dialogue about it. Many marriages carry with them vivid snapshots of past hurts. If you and your husband haven't communicated to the point of resolution about your communication breakdowns, continue opening the lines of communication by being direct and kind, choosing the proper time and place to speak, listening carefully to your husband, and having intentional dialogue.

You may be the tool God uses to unlock your husband's soul. What a privilege to be used by God in this way!

1. Are you direct in your communication? If not, why?
2. Have you ever misinterpreted something your husband communicated? What effect did this have on you? Your husband?
3. How would you rate your listening skills?
4. Do you deal with issues as they arise, or do you stuff them away? What is the cause of your procrastination? What feelings do you experience when you put off communication?
5. When you communicate about an issue, are you kind? If not, is this working for you?
6. Have you ever chosen an improper time and/or place to communicate with your husband? What was the result?

1. Instead of telling your husband about your day, choose three specific questions to ask in the course of an evening that will draw him into conversation about his day. Be sure

that they're not questions that can be answered with one word. When he answers, practice mirroring, validating, and empathizing. Journal what you learn from this exercise.

2. Initiate an open, honest discussion with your husband about the communication within your marriage. Begin the conversation with the words, "I'd like your input," *not* "We need to talk!" Use the communication techniques discussed—Be direct, kind, choose the proper place and time, and listen to understand.

CHAPTER EIGHT

Speaking Truth in Love

❧

*Instead, we will speak the truth in love, growing in
every way more and more like Christ.*
—EPHESIANS 4:15 (NLT 2007)

*Apart from God . . . a marriage-saving
love is not within us.*
—MAX LUCADO, *A LOVE WORTH GIVING*

In *Hinds' Feet on High Places,* a little deer named Much Afraid
longs to leave her home in the village of Much-Trembling to go
to the High Places. The Good Shepherd has just told her that Sorrow
and Suffering would be her guides.

> "I can't go with them," she gasped. "I can't! I can't! O my Lord
> Shepherd, why do you do this to me? How can I travel in their
> company? It is more than I can bear. You tell me that the moun-
> tain way itself is so steep and difficult that I cannot climb it
> alone. Then why oh why, must you make Sorrow and Suffering
> my companions? Couldn't you have given Joy and Peace to go
> with me on the difficult way? I never thought you would do this
> to me!" And she burst into tears.
>
> Sorrow and Suffering had always seemed to her the two
> most terrifying things which she could encounter. How could
> she go with them and abandon herself to their power and

control? It was impossible. Then she looked at the Shepherd and suddenly knew she could not doubt him, could not possibly turn back from following him; that if she were unfit and unable to love anyone else in the world, yet in her trembling, miserable little heart, she did love him. Even if he asked the impossible, she could not refuse.

She looked at him piteously, then said, "Do I wish to turn back? O Shepherd, to whom should I go? In all the world I have no one but you. Help me to follow you, even though it seems impossible. Help me to trust you as much as I long to love you."[1]

Do you find yourself in the company of sorrow and suffering in your marriage? What struggles are you facing—money mismanagement, faith differences, anger, addictions, parenting issues, pornography, unfaithfulness? Unfortunately, because we live in a fallen world, sorrow and suffering will be a part of every relationship at one time or another. Fortunately, God can use these things to bring us to the High Places. God uses sorrow and suffering to bring us into contact with new or previously undiscovered truths about Himself, and when we embrace these truths, our lives will be changed.

Would you like to see growth come out of your marital sorrow and suffering? Learn to identify truth, apply love, and speak assertively. Ephesians 4:15–16 (NIV) says,

Instead, speaking the truth in love, we will in all things grow up into him who is the Head, that is, Christ. From him the whole body, joined and held together by every supporting ligament, grows and builds itself up in love.

There are three things involved here—speaking, truth, and love—but they must not occur in that order! Speaking does not come first. When do you speak? When you have examined the truth and are prepared to act in love. Before you ever open your mouth, you must know God's truth concerning you and your husband. You must identify the truth before determining if there's a need to speak, and what you will say.

IDENTIFY THE TRUTH

Jesus said, "You are truly my disciples if you keep obeying my teachings. And you will know the truth, and the truth will set you free" (John 8:31–32). How do you identify the truth? Begin by asking yourself two questions: What is the truth about my husband's behavior? What is the truth about my behavior?

The Truth About Him

What is the truth about your husband's behavior? Are his sins contributing to your marriage problems?

Tom's sins caused me sorrow and suffering on a regular basis during the first eleven years of our marriage. When asked today, he speaks honestly about the sin that was in his life. He was emotionally abusive and controlling. When I didn't do something Tom's way, he punished me with verbal abuse or the silent treatment. He offered gifts and then withheld them when I didn't please him. He did his best to control whom I could see and when, what I could wear, and what I could eat.

The truth about these behaviors was that they were sinful. Tom was walking in disobedience to God and had, as Malachi 2:14 (NKJV) says, "dealt treacherously" with me. Are your husband's sins contributing to your marriage problems? *In the case of physical abuse, addictive behaviors, or emotional abuse, please remember that it is not your fault— seek professional help now.*

However, not all of the problems I have had with my husband involved his sin. Sometimes it is difficult for us women to distinguish between annoyances and sin.

I remember one weekend in particular when my husband was suffering from a cold. I watched him blow his nose and drop snotty tissues one after the other onto the wood floor. When he poured his coffee, it spilled onto the floor. I was more than annoyed. After several more tissues and coffee spills, I began to think about other aggravating behaviors of his. Before long, the steam building inside of me exploded at my sick husband. Poor guy.

In that situation, I don't think God was seriously concerned with Tom's behavior. My husband wasn't sinning—he was living. I should have let this go.

Consider your husband's behavior: is it sinful or just annoying? Studying God's Word will help you distinguish between the two. It benefits you to know the difference and let the annoying things go. If you regularly use your influence to spotlight annoyances, you'll have little influence left to address sin.

The Truth About You

How are you responding to your husband's sin? Are you stuck in a rut of ineffective, sinful behavior to get your husband's attention about his sin? Do you preach to your husband when he disobeys God? When he hurts you, do you withhold love or return evil for evil? Is your energy devoted to fixing him?

If you are solely focused on your husband's sin and how it is affecting you, chances are you are not looking at yourself long enough to determine if your methods in dealing with him are sinful. This is an easy trap to fall into because it's easier to see another person's faults than it is to deal with your own. Getting out of this trap will require an examination of your own life in the light of God's Word. "But when the light shines on them, it becomes clear how evil these things are. And where your light shines, it will expose their evil deeds" (Ephesians 5:13–14).

What is the truth about your behavior? Are your own sins contributing to your marriage problems? Many women never ask these questions, especially if they are feeling hurt. However, until you look long and hard at these questions, you may be standing in the way of progress, growth, and healing in your marriage. Take courage and look carefully at your behavior for the sake of your relationship with your husband.

When I looked at my actions in light of God's Word, I saw eleven years of ineffective and sinful behavior. I had been practicing a ruinous combination of preaching, dishonesty, withholding love, and returning evil for evil. Because I hadn't been looking at my own behavior, I couldn't see my sinful issues; all I could see were Tom's. Thus, I kept directing my energies toward fixing him, to no avail. If you think the solution to your marriage problems lies in changing your husband, you're headed for disappointment. You can only change yourself. I had heard this in pre-marriage counseling, but that didn't stop me from trying to change Tom.

When I was fighting for my marriage, I began seeing a Christian marriage counselor. She asked me to imagine three points on a line—one in the middle and one on each end. I was the point in the middle with Tom on one end and God on the other. From the middle, I was instructing my husband that his behavior was ungodly and therefore wouldn't be blessed. Then I'd look in the other direction and whine to God about how Tom was treating me. I was blocking Tom's view of God. God wanted that middle position, and I needed to move.

It wasn't until I allowed God to have the middle position—letting Him speak to Tom about his issues and to me about mine—that I experienced peace. It is a terrible burden, feeling responsible for changing someone else, and releasing that burden gave me peace. Any changes that God wanted to make in Tom were now His responsibility.

Obeying God's Truth

Once I wasn't in the middle of things, I could sense God leading me, through His Word, in a new direction. I searched His Word and found a few key verses to quote to myself often, verses that reminded me to stay on the path leading to a healthy marriage:

- "In the same way, you wives must accept the authority of your husbands, even those who refuse to accept the Good News. Your godly lives will speak to them *better than any words*. They will be won over by watching your pure, godly behavior"

(1 Peter 3:1–2, emphasis mine). In place of preaching at Tom, I began to live out my faith in God, entrusting my difficult situation to Him through prayer.

+ "Instead, we will hold to the truth in love, becoming more and more in every way like Christ" (Ephesians 4:15). I began to replace preaching with speaking the truth in love—in as few words as possible.

+ "See that no one pays back evil for evil, but always try to do good to each other and to everyone else" (1 Thessalonians 5:15). On my new path, I chose kindness in place of angry retaliation.

I experienced a new freedom on this path, but the way was still difficult. It was difficult to respond in love to Tom when his behavior was unloving, but obeying God in this brought me personal blessing. There was never a day that I didn't experience His presence through His Word, a devotional, or the love of a friend. I had never felt closer to my Lord. He was with me, encouraging me every step of the way.

Ephesians 3:20 was particularly encouraging: "Now glory be to God! By his mighty power at work within us, he is able to accomplish infinitely more than we would ever dare to ask or hope." When I felt discouraged, I reminded myself that leaving Tom in God's hands would accomplish infinitely more than I could hope for and that trying to change him myself had never accomplished even the smallest true reform.

Seek God's truth by reading the Bible. As you do, compare your actions to His ways. It will become clear if personal behavior changes are needed. Ask the Holy Spirit to reveal to you how to apply the truth that you find. The Bible doesn't lay out exact instructions for every situation you encounter, but the Holy Spirit can advise you. As you pray about how to proceed, you will sense the Spirit's direction.

One of my favorite prayers is, "Help, God!" He will not withhold wisdom from those who ask Him how to apply His Word. On the contrary, He delights in this request. It's no different than if your child said, "Mom, I want to obey you. Can you tell me how to obey you better?" Wouldn't you be thrilled to provide guidance to this child? God delights in a teachable heart and provides His Spirit to live in us and to counsel us. "If you need wisdom—if you want to know what God wants you to do—ask him, and he will gladly tell you" (James 1:5).

Also, seek counsel from a wise Christian woman or a Christian counselor as I did. You will receive critical help and support needed to identify and obey God's truth. "Without counsel plans go wrong, but with many advisers they succeed" (Proverbs 15:22 RSV).

You can also find this support in a Beautiful Womanhood small group or another marriage support group. There, you will meet other women facing problems just like yours! You will have the support of your peers and your mentor, and the opportunity to discuss God's truth on topics relevant to your marriage.

When I stopped trying to change my husband and shifted my focus to obeying God's truth concerning my own issues, I paved the way for speaking the truth in love about his sinful behaviors.

IN LOVE

"If I could speak in any language in heaven or on earth but didn't love others, I would only be making meaningless noise like a loud gong or a clanging cymbal" (1 Corinthians 13:1). If you wish to accomplish more than making an irritating racket in your husband's ears, you will need to combine the truth with love before speaking.

God's definition of love is found in 1 Corinthians 13:4–7:

Love is patient and kind. Love is not jealous or boastful or proud or rude. Love does not demand its own way. Love is not irritable, and it keeps no record of when it has been wronged. It is never glad about injustice but rejoices whenever the truth wins out. Love never gives up, never loses faith, is always hopeful, and endures through every circumstance.

This is how God loves us, and since He calls us to be like Him in every way, He calls us to love others the way He has loved us.

God Loves You

It's strange but true; we can learn in Sunday school all the beliefs of the kingdom of God, but we will spend the rest of our lives learning what they really mean. "God loves me"—it's the greatest truth. It's the easiest and most difficult thing to learn.

A woman I know shared that, for a time, she asked God daily to teach her how much He loved her. She prayed Paul's prayer for the Ephesians for herself: that she would comprehend how immense God's love was for her and know His love in a way that went beyond mental comprehension so she would be filled with the fullness of God (Ephesians 3:14–19). She asked Him to carve out more space in her heart for Him so that she could hold more of His love. She often waited on her couch until she felt His love, and then she waited again, letting His love flood her until she felt she could burst with it.

Do you struggle knowing how to tap into God's love? When you read the Bible, do you read the words with such self-condemnation that you hear only judgment? When you do tap into God's love, do you linger until your heart feels like it could burst, or do you leave after the first taste, satisfied with a teaspoonful when He desires to give you a truckload?

Regularly reading God's love letter—the Bible—enlarges our understanding of how much He loves us. I often read a little booklet, "Who I Am in Christ," which reminds me of how much I am loved by my Father God.[2] If you're feeling low on love, recite these verses to yourself:

And this expectation will not disappoint us. For we know how dearly God loves us, because he has given us the Holy Spirit to fill our hearts with his love. (Romans 5:5)

Instead, be kind to each other, tenderhearted, forgiving one another, just as God through Christ has forgiven you. (Ephesians 4:32)

For I can do everything with the help of Christ who gives me
the strength I need. (Philippians 4:13)

After filling up with God's love, you can give love to your husband
out of the overflow.

Exchange Your Pain for God's Love

When you are hurt by your husband, the pain goes deep.
Wounds caused by someone you love can be devastating. What
should you do with that kind of pain? Psalm 55:22 tells us to "Give
your burdens to the LORD, and he will take care of you. He will not
permit the godly to slip and fall." He will take your burdens when
you bring them to Him, but He doesn't want you to go away empty-
handed. He wants you to exchange your pain for His love. Once
you are filled with His love, you'll have something precious to give
to your husband.

I remember an occasion when my husband harshly criticized
something I had done for him. I fled into the bathroom, pouring
my heart out to God through tears, asking Him for His help. All at
once, I was overcome with His love for my husband. I was inspired to
go back to Tom and put my arms around him, telling him that God
loved him and so did I.

In *A Love Worth Giving*, Max Lucado reveals that the secret to
loving others is first receiving it from God. So before showing love to
our husbands, we should never skip the step of first turning toward
God and basking in His love for us. Without God's help we can't love
our husbands anyway.[3] As the apostle John says: "We love, because
he first loved us" (1 John 4:19 NASB). When I exchanged my pain for
God's love, I possessed a gift of infinite value that I could pass on to
my husband. God desires that you receive His love in order to give it
away.

It's a choice—a discipline—to systematically bring your pain to
God in exchange for His love that, in turn, is given away. It is hard
work, but it's worth the effort. Luke 6:38 says:

If you give, you will receive. Your gift will return to you in full measure, pressed down, shaken together to make room for more, and running over. Whatever measure you use in giving—large or small—it will be used to measure what is given back to you.

That's what I call return on investment! Receive all the love you can from God and give it all away. His supply is never depleted. Keep going back for more. His great desire is that you will.

Putting Love into Action

Once you have learned how to receive God's love in abundance, you need to pour out that love on your husband by putting it into action.

The first step is to forgive. Husbands and wives hurt each other; it's a natural consequence of intimacy between imperfect beings. Do you keep a record of wrongs against your husband? Do patience and kindness fly out the window when your expectations go unmet? We simply cannot afford to carry yesterday's offenses into today. We need to love each other with God's love, which keeps no record of wrongs. Forgiving our husbands becomes much easier when we regularly confess our own sins to God and experience His forgiveness. "If you forgive others, you will be forgiven. . . . But a person who is forgiven little shows only little love" (Luke 6:37; 7:47).

The act of forgiveness isn't the same thing as excusing sin. As long as you withhold forgiveness, you carry the offender and the offense with you; forgiveness releases you from that weighty burden. If you refuse to forgive over a long period of time, the offense grows into bitterness—which affects not only your spiritual condition but your physical health as well. Forgiveness is a blessing to *you!*

Second, remind yourself why you loved your husband in the first place. Keep a list of his positive qualities and the kind things he's done for you in the past. Reflect on these before approaching him with your loving truth.

Third, find concrete and small ways to show love to your husband each day. Loving someone who has wronged you can have a profound effect on them. Romans 12:21 says that we conquer evil by doing good. When I responded to Tom with love, I witnessed the fruit of this in my marriage. Tom's heart toward me gradually softened as I loved him with the love I received from the Father, a love that covered sins and conquered evil.

Now that you've found the truth and combined it with love, it's time to speak.

SPEAKING

You must speak the truth in love, if the truth about your husband involves sin—not just annoyances. Once you know the truth and you're full of love, the third part of speaking the truth in love is speaking. Sounds easy, right? The trick is knowing *how* to speak. The way in which you communicate the loving truth will often determine whether or not your husband will hear you. Psychologists commonly distinguish between four basic types of communication or behavior: passive, aggressive, passive-aggressive, and assertive. Only one is healthy.

Passive Behavior

The dictionary defines the word *passive* as "receiving or enduring without resistance," and "existing without being active."[4] Do you endure your husband's sinful behavior without ever saying a word? If so, he may not know what you think or feel about his sinful actions because you haven't shared your thoughts. You may think your husband is a mind reader, but he is not!

Dishonesty. Perhaps you communicate passively by lying about your true feelings. You may hint at your disagreement but never clearly state your true feelings. You may pretend to understand when you don't. You may lie to him to avoid his anger or criticism.

Silence. Passive people tend to prize peace and acceptance above truth, so they remain silent, usually suffering on the inside. This is a dangerous and ineffective path to take.

When you withhold vital feedback, you turn a blind eye to the danger your husband is in. He will go unchecked if he assumes you are in agreement with his behavior. And if you're not in agreement, anger and resentment will build in you as he continues in his sin. Anger and resentment will not give you the peace your passive heart desires. You must press past your pain and fear of confrontation in order to help your husband experience true freedom. Remember, "God has not given us a spirit of fear and timidity, but of power, love, and self-discipline" (2 Timothy 1:7).

Aggressive Behavior

Aggressive people are "marked by combative readiness."[5] Are you always ready to pick a fight, disregarding others' rights in pursuit of your own needs? In order to point out your husband's sin, do you walk all over him?

Insults and Profanity. An aggressive woman attacks in a cruel and insensitive manner when it comes to communicating to her husband about his sinful actions. She uses insults and put-downs, and might use profanity to express herself. She lets hurt and fear pour out in a torrent of anger. Abandoning self-control, she holds nothing back. Nothing is sacred.

Blame and Sarcasm. The aggressive woman wants to point the finger of blame, and she often does so in front of others. She may use sarcasm to make her point, either in a cutting way, or to pass her words off as a "joke." Saying, "If we were all as good with handling money as my husband is, we'd all be broke in no time," is a hurtful way to gain your husband's attention about poor money management. Belittling your husband will not accomplish what the aggressive woman desires—which is to have the problem resolved.

"Some people make cutting remarks," says Proverbs 12:18, "but the words of the wise bring healing." How does cutting aggressiveness affect your husband? He'll either become your opponent or a wimp. Some men retaliate with aggressive behavior of their own, and some men wilt or back away. Your disrespectful behavior will press him one way or the other.

Passive-Aggressive Behavior

"Individuals who use passive aggression are sometimes called 'powerful passives' because they use undercover ways to get their way, to get even, and to express what they are not willing to say in a straightforward manner."[6] A passive-aggressive woman makes jokes or snide remarks to draw her husband into conversation about his behavior. She procrastinates, forgets, and dawdles in order to convey displeasure without saying why. Do you pout and then deny that anything is bothering you when your husband inquires? If so, you struggle with passive-aggressive tendencies. This behavior is not honest.

Jokes and Snide Remarks. Do you ever make jokes or snide remarks about something that's bothering you concerning your husband? If you make a nasty comment about your husband's lack of honesty, for example, and afterward say, "I'm just kidding," you're probably not, and your husband knows it. Many a woman passes off her comments as "kidding" instead of assertively discussing her concerns with her husband.

Forgetfulness. Do you convey your displeasure with your husband through convenient forgetfulness?

During the difficult years of our marriage, Tom would ask me to do things for him, and when I was angry about something he'd done, I'd "forget" to do the requested task. It was easier to be dishonest and claim I'd forgotten it, rather than to confront Tom with my feelings. Interestingly, the message he heard was that he wasn't important to me because I frequently "forgot" what was important to him. The message I wanted him to hear was I was hurt.

Silent Treatment. The passive-aggressive woman uses the silent treatment. She punishes her husband by ignoring his existence without telling him why. She finds it far easier to punish him indirectly than to confront him honestly.

When I was hurt by Tom, I often used the silent treatment to send a signal to him that I was in emotional pain. My plan was for him to see my pain, be moved by it, and act to heal me. As I reflect back, I find it laughable that I thought silence was effectively communicating my heart to Tom. In reality, the silent treatment shut down all communication.

How does passive-aggressive behavior affect your husband? It confuses him. He wonders what he's done that has upset you. He senses your displeasure but can't make sense of it, much less "fix" it. All he has to work with are your dishonest or unclear messages, rather than clear explanations. You must speak truthfully with your husband in order to be understood.

Assertive Behavior

Passive, aggressive, and passive-aggressive methods are not effective. Only assertive behavior can bring healing to your marriage. Whether you are dealing with everyday issues or sinful behavior, always try to speak assertively. Assertive behavior "reflects concern about being honest, direct, open, and natural in relations with others."[7] An assertive woman utilizes honesty, respect, and patience when speaking to her husband for his benefit as well as for her own.

Honesty. Is being direct or honest as difficult for you as it is for me and many others?

When I saw Tom's sinful behavior, it was difficult for me to show concern for him by using a direct approach in my communication. I was afraid if I was straightforward about my concerns, he would become angry with me for exposing his sin and would reject me by distancing himself from me emotionally.

We who have a fear of rejection find it difficult to work up the courage to speak honestly to our husbands because our self-worth depends on others' approval. It is at this point we must remind ourselves that selfishness—meeting our own needs at the expense of someone else's—does nothing for our self-worth. Which is more important: your need for acceptance or your husband's need for the truth? His relationships with the Lord, with you, and with your children may suffer long-term if his sin goes unchecked. Aren't the welfare of these relationships worth the effort of overcoming our fears and speaking up?

Speaking with honesty increases the likelihood that your husband will actually hear you. He won't hear your concern through a series of hints. Unlike women, men aren't typically wired to detect hidden meanings and subtleties. They depend on us to be clear when we want them to know something.

When I began to speak the truth in love to my husband, I used this model: "I feel _____ when you _____." For example, when Tom was angry with me, made cutting remarks, and used profanity, I would say: "I feel frightened and hurt when you degrade me and curse at me." With a focus on straightforward honesty, the words "degrade" and "curse" got to the heart of the matter. Then, I would walk away, lest I be drawn into a fight with him and undo the good I had done. It was more effective leaving him alone with the truth ringing in his ears.

By the way, this is also a helpful model to follow for reinforcing the positive seeds your husband sows into your marriage. Rather than nagging about what he doesn't do, highlight the positive things he does. Use words such as, "I feel comforted when you _____" or "I feel cherished when you _____."

I do my best to live by my marriage creed, which concludes, "Two people can accomplish more than twice as much as one; they get a better return for their labor. If one person falls, the other can reach out and help. But people who are alone when they fall are in real trouble" (Ecclesiastes 4:9–10). Has your husband fallen into sinful behavior? Is he in trouble? I exhort you to reach out and help him by speaking with honesty. Push past your fear for the sake of him who clearly needs to hear the truth.

Respect. Straightforward honesty is important, but without respect, the truth you speak won't be received well by anyone. Communicating with respect is critical if you want your husband to hear your concern.

When the apostle Paul told us to respect our husbands (Ephesians 5:33), he didn't give us a loophole for husbands who don't deserve respect. We must respect our husbands. Period. If your husband doesn't deserve your respect, yet you choose to obey God's call and give it anyway, God will use your obedience for your good and His glory. Moreover, when you offer respect to a husband who is walking in sin, you offer a great gift of love, the kind of love God offers you. "Most important of all continue to show deep love for each other, for love covers a multitude of sins" (1 Peter 4:8).

Mold your body language to express respect. Your stance should be as open and vulnerable as you can manage. Face your husband and look into his eyes. Try not to cross your arms when talking or pull away if he tries to touch you or pull you to him in love.

Is your tone respectful? Try taking deep breaths to calm yourself, so you can speak calmly and normally rather than shouting. Deliberately add compassion and respect to your tone.

Out of respect for Tom, I focused on communicating my feelings when I confronted him. I didn't attack Tom or his character by saying, "You always _____" or "You never _____." Instead of criticizing him in a spirit of judgment, I vulnerably showed him my heart in a spirit of humility. Humility suggests an attitude of respect.

When you say, "I feel _____ when you _____," you highlight how your husband's actions affect you, not what you think of his actions. These words do not convey judgment or punishment. They do not attack him; they reveal how you feel. Consequently, they diminish the chance that he'll feel threatened and increase the chance he'll feel respected—because in the midst of a painful situation, you are trusting him with your feelings.

What is it you feel when your husband behaves sinfully? Consider your answer carefully, and be ready to share it with him when it's appropriate. Words such as *hurt*, *frightened*, or *abandoned*, paint him a picture of how his sinful behavior affects you, without being disrespectful in the process. With respect in mind, I also implemented a piece of advice a Christian counselor gave me—use ten words or less when confronting your husband. That was indeed a challenge! Preaching to your husband is ineffective because he interprets preaching as you telling him what to do, which he translates as disrespect. Your motive is right—sharing God's Word out of concern for him—but your method is wrong. As we've already seen in 1 Peter 3:1–2, it's ultimately our godly lives that win our husbands over, not our words. Husbands feel disrespected when we start preaching.

In addition to speaking to our husbands with respect, we need to also be careful to speak *about* them respectfully. Out of respect for your husband, avoid sharing details concerning your marriage struggles with your parents. It is difficult for even well-intentioned Christian parents to refrain from taking sides when they hear how "that man" is hurting their daughter. Painful details are hard for parents to forget. Whenever possible, marriage struggles are best discussed with godly women outside close family circles. They can point you to God and His wisdom, without the trappings of familial bias. This is a safeguard for your husband's future relations with your parents.

Patience. I have news for you: even after delivering the truth with love, you will rarely see instantaneous change in your husband. When speaking assertively, patience is an important attribute. When I was younger, I needed to see immediate change, but over time I have grown in my ability to live without resolution.

Do you push your husband into a corner, forcing his agreement or behavior change? The next time you lovingly speak the truth, walk away without expecting immediate results. Give God time to work. He is in charge of the results—not you. Jesus said, "Apart from me you can do nothing" (John 15:5). Leave the work of conviction, change, and outcomes to God.

You will also need to apply patience when your husband has had a bad day. If his stress and tension have nothing to do with you, don't take his frustration personally. Cut him some slack. This is not the time to speak the truth about his actions. Give him grace and love; he needs that more than ever when things have not gone smoothly for him. Use the same measure of patience toward him that you would like applied to you.

PUTTING IT ALL TOGETHER

When you speak the truth in love using honesty, respect, and patience, your husband will be able to understand your concerns and see the results of his actions. Then he will be in a position to make a choice about those actions.

Assertively speaking the truth in love caused a dramatic change in my marriage. On one occasion, after telling Tom how his actions affected me, he drew me to him, holding me tight, apologizing through many tears. This was not always his response. At other times, he was angry as he came face-to-face with the effects of his sinful behavior. He was faced with it—not because I was throwing it into his face—but because I wasn't standing in the way any longer. He could clearly see the results of his own actions.

In the midst of Tom's sorrow or anger, I was at peace. I was no longer responsible for making the changes in Tom's life—it was up to God. And He was up to the task! His promise proved true: "By his mighty power at work within us, he is able to accomplish infinitely more than we would ever dare to ask or hope" (Ephesians 3:20).

God performed a miracle in our marriage as He was given free rein to work in both of us individually. I learned to speak the truth in love when I was mistreated, rather than preaching, retaliating in anger, or returning evil for evil. Later, through the counsel of a godly man, Tom realized he was dealing treacherously with me and was convicted that

I was a gift from God designed especially for him. He began putting my needs before his own and living kindly and considerately of me, instead of criticizing me. As a sign of the new changes taking place in him, Tom lined me and our children up on the couch one evening and washed our feet! He declared that he was choosing to be a servant-leader in our home—no longer an angry, controlling man.

What stood between me and this marvelous act of God those first eleven years? Me. I found I was part of the problem. I had been handling things my own way instead of allowing God to direct my marriage. I was too busy focusing on Tom and his sin, instead of on God and what He was speaking to me through His Word. Having found and submitted to God's truth, the truth set me free.

It's important to distinguish that it wasn't what I did that made the difference in Tom's life and in our marriage, it was what *God did* through my obedience. He gave me freedom and peace in exchange for the futile expectation of trying to change another human being. He gave me the joy that comes from walking closely with Him and doing something right and pleasing in His sight.

I don't know how God will work in your marriage when you allow Him to direct you, but you can trust Him. Your experience may look different from mine, but I can guarantee this: obeying God will be a blessing to *you*. No matter what your husband chooses, you will experience fulfillment when you focus on God.

If you speak the truth in love in the face of great difficulty in your marriage, get ready for God's blessing. It will come. You will be blessed for your obedience to Him no matter how your husband chooses to respond. Your honor for God through obedience to His Word will bring great blessing on your life, if not your marriage.

The little deer, Much Afraid, did allow Sorrow and Suffering to be her guides to the High Places, and when she arrived, the Good Shepherd changed her name to Grace and Glory.

"Grace and Glory, . . . do you think you understand now how I was able to make your feet like hinds' feet and to set you on these High Places?" . . .

[Grace and Glory said,] "Every circumstance in life, no matter how crooked and distorted and ugly it appears to be, if it is reacted to in love and forgiveness and obedience to your will can be transformed. Therefore, I begin to think, my Lord, that you purposely allow us to be brought into contact with the bad and evil things that you want changed. . . .

Perhaps that is the very reason why we are here in this world, where sin and sorrow and suffering and evil abound, so that we may let you teach us how to react to them, that out of them we can create lovely qualities to live forever. That is the only really satisfactory way of dealing with evil, not simply binding it so that it cannot work harm, but whenever possible overcoming it with good."[8]

Do you have an opportunity in your marriage to overcome evil with good? If and when you do, choose to speak the truth in love, and God will lead *you* to the High Places!

— *Reflection* —

1. Recall a recent marriage problem. How did you respond? Did it involve a sinful behavior, or an annoyance?
2. Which one of the verses quoted in this chapter resonates with you the most?
3. With whom could you talk to get godly counsel?
4. If someone asked how your husband wrongs you, could you make a list? How does the list of wrongs affect your attitude toward your marriage?
5. When your expectations go unmet, how do you react? What impact does your reaction have on your relationship?
6. Which do you most often use: passive, aggressive, passive-

aggressive, or assertive communication? Is this working for you?

7. Which is most difficult for you: honesty, respect, or patience? Why?

8. What body language do you typically use to express anger, frustration, or hurt? The next time you find yourself doing these, what could you do instead?

9. When are you least likely to be patient with your husband? Why? What could you do or remember to help yourself be more patient the next time you feel impatient?

First Steps

1. Journal about a difficult marital issue you face. Address the following questions: Are your husband's actions sinful or simply annoying? Have you been responding to his actions with your own sinful behavior? (If so, go to God; ask forgiveness for yourself.) What can you do to fill up with God's love in order to give it to your husband? (Now, do it.)

2. After you have prayerfully completed First Step #1, you are ready to speak with honesty, respect, and patience about this difficult issue. Write out your plan for doing so, then implement it. After you do, journal a prayer, asking God for help in continuing on this new path of speaking the truth in love.

CHAPTER NINE

Managing Money

> The love of money is at the root of all kinds of evil.
> And some people, craving money,
> have wandered from the faith
> and pierced themselves with many sorrows.
>
> —1 Timothy 6:10

> It's not how much you make that matters;
> it's what you do with what you have.
>
> —Mary Hunt,
> *Debt-Proof Your Marriage*

*L*ike many couples, Tom and I entered marriage having never discussed a plan for dealing with finances. Yet, we came from different backgrounds and had different ideas about how money should be spent. As a couple, if you don't work together to create a plan for spending money, you will likely fight over the money you spend, fall far short of your financial goals, and forsake the intimacy that working together toward a common goal provides. The saying holds true. "If you fail to plan, you plan to fail." Why not create a successful plan you both agree on?

Before drafting your plan, it's important to come to an understanding of what motivates your thoughts concerning money. Doing so will prove extremely beneficial when you understand the tendencies you'll need to resist or the disciplines you should enact in order to be a blessing to your husband financially.

Popular author and financial advisor Suze Orman said, "The road to financial freedom begins not in a bank or even in a financial planner's office, but in your head. It begins with your thoughts. And those thoughts, more often than not, stem from our seemingly forgotten past with money."[1] All of us come away from childhood with thoughts and attitudes about money—some good, some harmful. What has your past taught you about money? Which thoughts and attitudes did you learn while young that still govern the way you view your finances? Until you explore your thoughts and feelings about money, as Orman suggests, it will be difficult to experience the thrill of financial freedom and peace with your husband.

As an impressionable child, I formed many unhealthy attitudes about money that have hindered me as an adult. My parents lost thousands of dollars in a shady snack vending company. This investment-gone-bad brought increased tension, fear, and frustration into our home. A seed of fear rooted in my young heart: a fear of financial insecurity (as an adult, I still fear what a financial misstep might do to Tom, me, and our marriage).

Later, when my family of modest means moved to an affluent community, I learned to believe that money was the route to happiness and importance. At my school, the popular students wore clothes with certain labels, skied on weekends, and traveled south in the winter—I believed my lack of sufficient funds kept me from experiencing fun and prestige. When I earned my own money, I spent it on whatever I thought would boost my status and ego.

I still struggle to manage the tug-of-war resulting from these conflicting attitudes—restraining fear versus carefree abandon. So, I tend to be unstable when dealing with money. Because I didn't get to the bottom of my issues early on, I wasn't the blessing I might have been to my husband.

In order to move beyond your self-defeating thoughts and attitudes about money, you'll need to replace them with God's thoughts.

God wants you to experience the thrill of financial security by following His plan.

GOD'S FINANCIAL PLAN

Did you know there are over two thousand verses in the Bible on the subject of money and possessions? It tops the number of verses on prayer and faith combined! Robert Morris suggests that these numbers indicate the importance of our understanding about money and how to handle it. Why? "Because money is actually a test from God. How you handle money reveals volumes about your priorities, loyalties and affections. In fact, it directly dictates many of the blessings you will (or won't) experience in life."[2] What single most important fact must you know to pass this test that affects your financial future? God owns it all! Everything we have comes from God and belongs to Him.

I never really grasped the importance of God's ownership of my finances until I read Randy Alcorn's analogy of stewardship in *The Treasure Principle*.[3] You and I are God's money managers (stewards), and He is the owner. The qualities Tom and I look for in a money manager are a reputation for increasing wealth and strong moral character. We want to trust that he won't squander our money on his own selfish pursuits. When we willfully spend the money God entrusts to us on selfish pursuits, we become like the disreputable money manager who uses others' money to buy things for his own personal gain. When perpetrated against another person, this action is punishable by law—we should take it just as seriously when it is against God.

In Matthew 25, Jesus tells the story about a master who gave money to three servants to invest for him. The first two doubled their money while the master was away. When the master returned, he was overjoyed and promoted both of them. The third servant, however, had buried the money in the ground. Furious, the master rebuked this wicked servant, who'd been too lazy to even deposit the money in the bank to earn interest. The master took the money away from him and gave it to the first servant. Verse 29 sums up what God wants us to learn from this story: "To those who use well what they are given, even more will be given, and they will have an abundance. But from those who are unfaithful, even what little they have will be taken away."

When you see yourself in the role of money manager rather than owner, you realize you're not entitled to the money He's entrusted to you. You are to manage His assets wisely, always looking for the best place to invest in His kingdom. He wants you to increase what He's given you, provide for your needs, and provide for others' needs as well.

Giving

Giving is a godly principle. God practices and requires giving. John 3:16 reveals God's greatest gift to us—His Son—at a great cost. You are a beneficiary of this life-saving gift. God wants you to enjoy the pleasures of giving, too. Percentage, priority, and progressive giving are a part of His financial plan for you.

Percentage Giving. As the Owner, God asks you to begin by giving back to Him 10 percent (called a tithe) of everything He's entrusted you.

> "Bring all the tithes into the storehouse so there will be enough food in my Temple. If you do," says the LORD Almighty, "I will open the windows of heaven for you. I will pour out a blessing so great you won't have enough room to take it in! Try it! Let me prove it to you!" (Malachi 3:10)

You might be thinking, "But I don't have enough money to pay my bills as it is!" I've been there myself. God understands this might be difficult to believe, so He backs it up with a promise. This passage in Malachi is the only place in the Bible where God asks us to test Him. Imagine you testing God! He must be fairly confident in His ability to provide for your needs if He is willing to put His reputation on the line.

Tom and I decided early in our marriage to obey God's principle of tithing—giving 10 percent of our income to our local church. Though we were tempted to withhold the tithe when our finances were tight, we consistently gave God 10 percent and lived on 90 percent. Granted, we also needed to apply wisdom when using our 90 percent! A trip to the mall for a spending splurge hoping God will pick up the tab is an unfair test. He promises throughout the Bible to provide for our needs, not our insatiable desires.

Throughout the years of tithing, God has steadily increased our finances, meeting and exceeding our needs. God's math might not make sense to you now, but it will. Test Him!

Priority Giving. God not only asks for 10 percent, but for the *first* 10 percent. "Honor the LORD with your possessions, and with the first-fruits of all your increase" (Proverbs 3:9 NKJV). Why? Giving to God first displays your acknowledgment of His lordship and right to rule in your life. When you give the first tenth, you make a statement that He comes first and that you trust Him to provide for the rest of your bills. When you give before you know if you have enough to provide for the rest of your needs, you give your faith an opportunity to grow.

Make God your priority and give back to Him first.

Progressive Giving. I was challenged by yet another thought in *The Treasure Principle*: "God prospers me not to raise my standard of living, but to raise my standard of giving."[4] Wow! It's easy for us Americans to selfishly believe the financial increase we experience is to be spent on ourselves. When we direct the increase into our own laps rather than looking to see what the Owner wants us to do with the extra resources, we become unfaithful managers.

I should know. Over the years, our income has increased and, while we've increased our giving to a point, we haven't given in proportion to God's increased provision for us. I thought the increase was for my benefit, so I kept more than I needed.

Things began to change when I visited Africa for a women's conference. In an African slum, I witnessed tremendous need I had formerly only read about. I visited a school built by a humble Ugandan pastor for children orphaned by the AIDS pandemic. His desire to feed, educate, and train poor orphaned children so they could escape poverty's curse both inspired and humbled me. I longed to meet some of those needs.

Sadly, I couldn't give as I wished. Our self-focused money managing had tied up our extra funds in a mortgage and a loan against our equity (to finance the things we wanted to do and buy). This kept us from giving freely as opportunities presented themselves. It wasn't just Africa. It was all the ministries mailing me, asking for help to reach people with real needs. I was grieved that I couldn't help like I wanted.

No longer am I satisfied with "token" giving. I am overwhelmed by God's blessings in my life—especially in comparison to how little most women in Africa have—and I want to give more. I have found a sense of balance in Paul's letter to the Corinthians: "Of course, I don't mean you should give so much that you suffer from having too little. I only mean that there should be some equality. Right now you have plenty and can help them" (2 Corinthians 8:13–14).

Consider this inspirational example of progressive giving from Rick Warren (founder and pastor of Saddleback Church in Lake Forest, California) and his wife:

Kay and I became reverse tithers. When we got married 30 years ago, we began tithing 10%. Each year we would raise our tithe 1% to stretch our faith: 11% the first year, 12% the second year, 13% the third year. Every time I give, it breaks the grip of materialism in my life. Every time I give, it makes me more like Jesus. Every time I give, my heart grows bigger. And so now, we give away 90% and we live on 10%. That was actually the easy part, what to do with the money—just give it away, because I'm storing up treasures in heaven.[5]

As God increases your finances, you have the opportunity to give more—more than 10 percent.

God has an antidote for materialism—giving! Percentage, priority, and progressive giving wield power to break this American pandemic and meet the needs of those less fortunate.

Debt-Free

If you're anything like me, it is hard to face up to the truth about money. But as Christ tells us, it is the truth that sets us free (John 8:32)—free to live in joy, peace, and love rather than fear, anxiety, and selfishness.

The Bible includes some key verses on the subject of debt:

Owe no one anything. (Romans 13:8 NKJV)

Just as the rich rule the poor, so the borrower is servant to the lender. (Proverbs 22:7)

We've got a debt problem in America! "Research by the Federal Reserve indicates that household debt is at a record high relative to disposable income. Some analysts are concerned that this unprecedented level of debt might pose a risk to the financial health of American households."[6]

For me, debt didn't become a problem until Tom was generating a good income. For the first time, I possessed a credit card—which eventually became several. We enjoyed all the good things money provided and neglected the need to limit ourselves. In the back of my mind, the fear that the money might dry up some day niggled at me, but I kept spending. I was on a roll.

Why is it so easy to become entangled with debt? Because we want more than we can afford, and we want it *now!* What a childish attitude.

When Mary Hunt, founder of *Cheapskate Monthly*, was first married, she began applying for and receiving credit cards for everything from gasoline to department store purchases. Every time she got a new, shiny credit card, she felt as if she'd been handed cash totaling the card's limit. She also formed a habit of writing checks before there was money in the bank to cover them. Her banker husband eventually told her he'd lose his job if she didn't stop writing bad checks.

Like most bad habits, Mary couldn't—or wouldn't—stop spending until the pain of the consequences exceeded the pain of changing her habits. For Mary, that point came when she realized they were $100,000 in debt. Fearing that her husband would leave her when he found out, she fell on her knees and promised God she'd do anything to get out of debt. She did, and now she helps thousands of others get out of debt, too.[7]

No matter what your story, you can learn to live debt-free. You'll have to go against the grain of society to do it, but many have overcome destructive financial tendencies and accomplished this very thing. There are many resources available to help guide you toward getting out of debt—check the resources section in the back of this book for a few suggestions. The following are just a few tips other women have found helpful for avoiding—or escaping—the trap of consumer debt:

- Cut up your credit cards or use a card that requires full payment each month.
- Remove temptation. Avoid malls, cancel catalogs, evade eBay, block home shopping channels, and decline invitations to home party shows.
- End impulse buying—no, you don't want fries with your order! Impose a waiting period to think about a purchase.
- Find a financial accountability partner, someone who understands how important it is to you to improve your spending habits and financial responsibility, someone who will keep your spending habits confidential, be an encourager, and ask the hard questions, such as, "Are you sure you didn't buy something that you haven't told me?"[8]

Living under the load of debt sucks joy from your life. Living within your means brings great peace.

Contentment

Paul wrote, "Not that I complain of want; for I have learned, in whatever state I am, to be content" (Philippians 4:11 RSV). Tom often jokes it's clear Paul never lived in the state of Michigan during winter! Seriously though, contentment is another of God's financial principles: "Yet true religion with contentment is great wealth. . . . So if we have enough food and clothing, let us be content" (1 Timothy 6:6, 8).

Contentment is difficult to grasp in a materialistic society that doesn't know the meaning of the word *enough*. Is there ever enough food, clothing, home decor, jewelry, collector's items, toys, etc.? The media displays a constant stream of desires to seduce your conscious and subconscious mind into the hotbed of materialism. Indeed, it's difficult to be content living in America.

Comparison is the great enemy of contentment. Satan loves to direct your focus to what your neighbor has in order to stir up discontentment.

When my family moved to an affluent community, I noticed that I lacked what many of my classmates had. My blue-and-white polyester bell-bottoms bought at the local bargain basement department store were missing one important item—a Levi's label. Comparison created a vacuum within me that demanded to be filled.

I carried the same tendency toward discontentedness into my marriage. When my sisters-in-law furnished their homes with antiques, I wanted to do so, too. Since I was unable to afford to, I believed my home didn't measure up to the beauty of theirs. I was consumed with jealousy and dreamed of the day I'd have the means to buy, buy, buy!

Even though I'm older and have more, I'm still tempted to compare myself with others who have even more than I do. I covet what I don't have and sometimes throw pity parties for myself, or brainstorm how I can attain the object of my desire. Either way, I'm agitated or miserable.

Adjust Your Vision. Do you find yourself discontent? If so, I guarantee you are focusing on what you don't have rather than on what you do have. Do you want more contentment? You'll have to adjust your vision.

Most American women are selectively far-sighted. We see what our neighbor has, but often overlook God's provision in our own home, closet, or garage. There's a reason God commands us not to covet anything our neighbor owns. Our far-sightedness causes us to forget how good we've got it, even without designer labels or antiques.

This overdeveloped sense of our personal needs obscures our capacity to see the needs around us. We need to adjust our vision to focus on the people beyond our own little world who have far less than we do.

The UN Millennium project brings the "faces of poverty" into focus for us:

> More than one billion people in the world live on less than one dollar a day. In total, 2.7 billion struggle to survive on less than two dollars per day. Poverty in the developing world, however, goes far beyond income poverty. It means having to walk more than one mile every day simply to collect water and firewood; it means suffering diseases that were eradicated from rich countries decades ago. Every year eleven million children die—most under the age of five and more than six million from completely preventable causes like malaria, diarrhea and pneumonia.[9]

Give Thanks. In order to experience contentment, you must also learn to practice thanksgiving. Gratefulness increases contentment, because it makes an accounting of what we have rather than what we don't have—and the tally is always more than we would have thought.

Make it a daily practice to thank God for what He's given you: food, shelter, clothing, strength, health, friends, family, freedom, grace, salvation. The list can go on and on. God loves it when we come into His presence with thanksgiving.

Adjusting your vision and practicing thanksgiving are how you plant the seeds of contentment. As contentment grows, so will your peace, joy, and bank account.

PREPARE A SPENDING PLAN

To be a faithful steward of the money God has entrusted to you, you should start by making a spending plan. A spending plan (budget) is a plan for the coordination of your resources and expenditures. Mutual cooperation between you and your husband in the preparation of this plan is essential if you hope to succeed.

Financial guru Dave Ramsey, author of the best-selling *Total Money Makeover*, says, "There's no denying that men and women look at money differently. Remember that opposites tend to attract in marriage, so work together for maximum wisdom. When you have a budget that reflects both of your goals and ideals, you will experience fabulous unity in your marriage."[10]

Many couples I know (including Tom and me) work against each other when not on the same financial page. One spouse has that "frugal feeling," and the other is happily spending. When the frugal spouse sees the spending spouse spending, frugality often flies out the window! In the name of fairness or selective ignorance, one forsakes reason for insanity and starts overspending, too. Ultimately, everyone loses and eventually you find yourself deep in debt.

To get on the same page financially, either you or your husband must draw up a spending plan. Dave Ramsey uses "nerd" and "free spirit" to describe spouses.[11] The nerd is the spouse whose personality and strengths are usually given to organization and attention to detail—this is essential in balancing your income with your spending. However, it doesn't imply that the free spirit has to lie down and accept any ol' budget the nerd drafts. The nerd isn't in control, but rather should use his or her talents for the good of the marriage. Once the nerd has created the initial draft of the spending plan, the free spirit must determine whether it's doable. If not, they go back to the drawing board and determine together where they can make adjustments.

When creating a spending plan:

- Track your spending for a month.
- Determine leaks and whether your expenses exceed your income.
- Decide where you can cut back to live within your means without using credit.
- Build an emergency fund. You can start by having a garage sale or selling something. Put the proceeds in the emergency fund. Then begin to set aside money from each paycheck until you have enough saved to cover three to six months of living expenses.
- If you have debt (cars, credit cards), make sacrifices you both agree on in order to systematically tackle it. Choose whether to begin with high interest debt first or to pay off smaller debts and then apply that money to larger debts to create a "snowball" effect. Use whichever plan motivates you!

The first step toward eliminating financial tension in your marriage is to make and stick to a spending plan you and your husband agree on.

Pay Bills on Time

Between you and your husband, who is best suited to pay the monthly bills? Mutually determine who will fulfill this role based on facts, rather than assumptions or preferences.

Paying bills quickly became a source of tension between Tom and me. My dad paid the bills when I was growing up, so I assumed Tom would fulfill this "husband's role" with the same attention to detail my dad possessed. When the water was turned off because Tom hadn't paid the bill on time, I angrily and disrespectfully took over the job. That created a lot of tension.

My friend's husband assumed she would be the one to pay the

bills because of her father's expertise as a banker and because she had more time available for the task. My friend was a "free spirit," though, and she found all sorts of ways to misuse her assigned responsibility.

It is important to pay your bills on time for the health of your finances. If you are the person best suited for the job, take your role seriously. If your husband is the bill payer, do all you can to support him and show appreciation for the extra time it takes to perform this task. Gather the bills together in one place so he doesn't have to track them down. Thank him for his efforts. Reward him with a back rub or a cup of coffee!

Determine Your Financial Goals

Where do you want to be financially in five, ten, twenty years? What function do you want your money to perform? When you live according to a spending plan, systematically paying off debt and paying bills on time, you can begin to dream!

You may dream of buying a house or taking a special family vacation. Maybe your dream includes starting a business, paying your child's way through college, or donating to good causes dear to your heart. Whatever your goals, share them with your husband. Write them down and review them regularly to evaluate whether they've changed or not. Once you've written them down, devise a plan to reach them, including which sacrifices you're willing—and unwilling—to make throughout the process. Excitement builds when you discover money is a tool to help you reach your financial goals.

Dreaming together will bring you and your husband closer together. You'll never be one of those couples who eat at a restaurant in silence, with nothing to say to each other. Determining your financial goals replaces tension with mutual cooperation and excitement.

Care for Your Children

The decision of whether a mother should work outside the home or not is often a financial one. If you desire to stay home with your kids but you currently work outside the home, initiate an honest conversation with your husband about the possibility of change. Together, evaluate the pros and cons of working versus staying home. Calculate the costs associated with your job: childcare, wardrobe, parking, eating out. After cutting back wherever possible, is there still a shortfall between these costs and what you earn? You could next consider reducing the number of hours you work outside the home. Reduce strategically so that you also cut back on work-related costs.

Because I wanted to be home with our kids, Tom and I needed creativity to make the dollars stretch. We cut costs in several ways:

+ Owned one used car
+ Shopped garage sales for clothing and household items
+ Seldom ate out
+ Cooked with *More-with-Less Cookbook* by Doris Janzen Longacre
+ Took camping vacations
+ Had some date nights at home. We sent the kids to bed early, cooked a nice meal, and watched a favorite show
+ Had some date nights with other couples, eating a nice meal in each other's homes while allowing the kids time to play together

By today's standards, some might think we were roughing it, but we have the best memories of those days! Our grown children tell funny stories of the great lengths to which I went to save money. None of us feels cheated by the sacrifices we made.

If you plan to have children, talk now with your husband about whether or not you wish to stay home with the kids. Planning ahead allows time to prepare for an income adjustment and will eliminate the tension caused by unspoken desires.

GROWING THROUGH FINANCIAL CRISIS

If you have a financial crisis, God can work through it to bring you closer as a couple, as the following stories illustrate.

Kristi's Story

In February 2007, Paul and I were over $37,000 in debt, didn't have a budget, and were living with no peace when it came to our finances. God didn't drop the check in the mail to cover the need for our great financial distress, but what He did do was give us the desire and opportunity to learn to take control of our finances. We officially became debt-free for the first time in our twenty-two years of marriage in May 2008. During those fifteen months we found ourselves growing even closer together as a result of communicating about our finances in a new way. We were also living better and giving more. Now we are enjoying the peace that comes from truly being free from the curse of debt. We really grasped the concept: "You work too hard all your life to grow old with no financial provision." God definitely has shown us the vision to leave an inheritance for our children's children and be givers!

Not only have I found that a shared vision for our finances has ignited a closer unity in our marriage, but I discovered a greater admiration for my husband because of his desire to lead us into financial freedom. This has now become our passion and has created an opportunity for us to minister to others in this area.

Marsha's Story

Our marriage was silently being suffocated by unresolved financial differences. I handled the finances, while Jeff made the money. He wanted nothing to do with the details of paying the bills, so they landed in my lap by default. I drudged through the mountain of bills alone for years. I dreaded facing it as we sunk deeper into debt. It seemed like we just couldn't get ahead. I read books on finances and wrote up a few budgets. But a budget won't work if only one person prepares it and is the only one using it. Deep down I knew we could never have victory in our finances until we became a united front.

Then Jeff started to despise credit cards, going further into debt, and the bondage it brought. Sometimes you have to get fed up with a situation before you find the motivation to seek outside help and change directions. So we signed up for the Dave Ramsey class at church. Together we confronted the mess we had created. Each week we gained new insight. We were learning and growing together. The class was much more fun than either of us had imagined! We did our homework together, created a budget together, and made financial decisions together. The heavy burden I had felt for all those years began to lift as we confronted our situation together. There was an added surprise, too. Not only were our finances turning around for good, but we were having more fun together—our relationship started to grow and flourish again.

I found 1 Timothy 6:6–8, which talks about godliness being a means of great gain when accompanied by contentment and that if we have food and covering, we shall be content. It gave me a reality check and a new aversion to spending money. Things I used to think I needed weren't things I needed at all. It was amazing how much money we saved this way. Being content with what I already had brought a tremendous freedom and great peace.

Jeff still likes to make the money, and I still do the bills. The big difference now is that we decide together where our money should go. We sit down as a team and discuss options and plans for the upcoming days, weeks, and years. It's a far better way of doing things—and a lot more fun!

If you and your husband are unable to get on the same financial page, you may need the help of a financial advisor. Contact your local church for recommendations. Christian marriage counseling may be in order to get at the root of overspending or addictive behaviors such as gambling. If your husband has a spending problem and refuses help, it may become necessary to talk to a lawyer about protecting yourself from ever-increasing debt. You may want to bring a pastor or church leader to help you confront a husband about a destructive spending behavior. Ask friends to pray for you as you struggle with this difficult issue.

God carefully watches what we do with the money He has entrusted us with. Throughout the Bible, He instructs us to take care of the poor, widows, and orphans. Are we listening and heeding His words?

Since 2007, Tom and I have been actively downsizing and biblically rightsizing our lifestyle so that we can be vessels through which God pours His vast resources—and not keep for ourselves. We are focused on laying up treasures in heaven rather than here on earth, remembering that our time on earth is no longer than the blink of an eye compared to the eternity we'll enjoy in heaven. We've been challenged by the command to "love your neighbor as yourself" (Matthew 19:19) and balance the lopsided scale of what we keep compared to what we give. Obedience to His Word is producing much joy in our souls!

Wouldn't the world be a better place if Christians everywhere obeyed God concerning their finances? Test Him, and see if He won't open the windows of heaven and pour out a blessing you cannot contain!

1. Which of your thoughts about money were formed in your past? Write them in your prayer journal. How have they affected your marriage?
2. Is the idea of God's ownership of your finances new to you? How does this knowledge affect the way you view spending? Journal a response.
3. What obstacle keeps you and your husband from tithing? What can you do to move past this obstacle?

4. Have you and your husband created an overall financial plan? If so, how has it affected your marriage? If not, how has your marriage been affected?

5. Are you currently living with a plan for your spending? If not, what helps you control spending?

6. Who is better with numbers, you or your husband? Is this the person handling the finances? Why, or why not?

7. If you work outside the home, would you prefer to stay home with your children until they begin attending school? If so, what has stopped you? Talk with your husband about what sacrifices could be made in order for you to stay home with your young children.

First Steps

1. Track your spending for a week (every cent!) and then examine your list. Are there areas where you could cut back and consequently give more generously to those in need? If so, pray with your husband about where God would direct your giving.

2. If you haven't developed a spending plan, tell your husband you would like the financial accountability that one provides. Explain your desire to work as a team to eliminate debt and build wealth. Express your excitement to dream together about your financial future and to give back to God 10 percent of all that He gives. Suggest changes you are willing to make if you desire to stay home with your kids.

3. If you don't currently contribute to the family income, discuss with your husband whether your financial contribution would relieve stress on him and thereby build greater unity in your marriage. Brainstorm ways that you could add to the family income, and discuss the pros and cons of each.

CHAPTER TEN

Creating a Culture of Beauty

> She carefully watches all that goes on in her household.
> —PROVERBS 31:27

> *If you ignore beauty, you will soon find yourself*
> *without it. . . . But if you invest in beauty, it will*
> *remain with you all the days of your life.*
> —FRANK LLOYD WRIGHT

God speaks to our hearts through beauty. Have you ever gazed on the mountains and felt your heart swell? Sat beside the ocean and found yourself thinking about God? Walked through a forest and thought new thoughts? During a vacation in 2001, my sister-in-law and I were overwhelmed with the beauty of the countryside, which led us to reflect on the beauty of our relationship. Before we knew it, we were developing a plan to provide a place for our married daughters to experience the same kind of love and support we had experienced together. Thus, the Beautiful Womanhood ministry was born.

God loves to create beauty—just look at the flowers or a sunset. "The heavens tell of the glory of God. The skies display his marvelous craftsmanship" (Psalm 19:1). You were made in His image (Genesis 1:27), so you share His love for beauty and His ability to create it.

Creating a culture of beauty in your home provides a place of refuge from the storms of life for you and your family, as well as a host of other uplifting benefits. In a 2002 *Focus on the Family* broadcast, Jean Lush said, "Beauty is energy creating." She went on to explain that beauty draws us to God. Beauty inspires. Beauty causes us to reflect. Beauty lifts the spirit, renews us with hope, and fills us with energy.

Your husband and children will be blessed by the beauty they see and feel in your home. However, your influence doesn't have to stop there. The culture of beauty in your home holds potential to bless anyone who walks through your front (or back) door.

There is a hurting world outside your home and you have a unique opportunity to touch the lives of your child's friends, co-workers, extended family members, and others to whom you're purposefully ministering. The love and beauty they see and feel in your home can put their soul at ease, make them feel as though they belong, and give them hope. Creating a culture of beauty is a tangible way to share Christ's love.

BEAUTY'S EXPRESSION

How do you demonstrate physical beauty in your home? Is there a particular design or motif you gravitate toward when buying home decor items? Which adjectives would you use to describe the particular look or style you use to decorate your home? If the descriptions that come to mind are similar to Yard-Sale Special, Toys "R" Us, or Worn & Threadbare, take a moment to mentally erase what is there and replace it with what you'd like to see. Now, how do you describe that style?

Each of us is drawn toward a particular decorating style. Identifying your style will help you to express beauty in your home. Chris Casson Madden, author of fourteen books and host of HGTV's *Interiors by Design*, has identified, through research and interviews with women, what she considers to be the three most prominent decorating styles: romantic, adventurous, and serene.

The romantic style combines country, cottage, and traditional decorating styles in unique ways. Women who fit the adventurous style prefer a decor with an eclectic assortment of accessories and art from different cultures and time periods. The serene style draws those who enjoy calm, neutral spaces or have a preference for a modern look.[1] Do you connect with any of these descriptions, or do you possess a style all your own?

Even when I shopped exclusively at garage sales and Goodwill, I was a romantic at heart. My home didn't look exactly like I wanted it to, but whenever possible I expressed my personal style as a romantic. Two words describe how I express beauty: *faded elegance.* I love grand, old objects with chipped paint. I find my favorite things at antique shops and garage sales. I live with and use these finds on a daily basis.

Anne defines her style as *warm modern.* She transformed her bathroom by painting the walls and ceiling black and stenciling tan diamonds on the ceiling. She added tan cabinets, loads of candles, soft lighting, and a shaggy bath mat. Finally, she completed the look with a piece of art made by her sister.

After a Beautiful Womanhood seminar, Pam described her home to me. She asked me what term I'd use to describe a room that was completely decorated around a deer's head! I laughed and said that was the *lodge look!*

What is your personal expression of beauty?

Uniquely You

Does your home reflect who you are, what you love, and the way you really live? Knowing yourself is the first step to defining your expression of beauty.

We're all different and have singular tastes. Our homes should express our individuality—and not look like cookie-cutter replicas of one other. Years ago, women I knew went to home decor parties, ordered the same items, and arranged them in similar formation on the walls—leaving little room for individuality. Instead of just copying your friends, get in touch with and express your uniqueness within the confines of a spending plan that you and your husband agree upon.

Defining Your Expression

What things do you cherish? I cherish my great-grandmother's china and old, black-and-white family pictures. This goes right along with a romantic, faded elegance. Anne cherishes her sister's artwork and uncluttered spaces. Granted, Pam may not cherish her husband's hunting trophy as much as he does, but sometimes compromise is in order. Your home should be a place where both you and your husband feel comfortable.

What inspires you?

- *Color.* Are you inspired by warm, deep colors or the light reflected from a serene white wall? Do you consistently gravitate toward a particular color? I found it interesting to discover that my living and dining room walls are painted in the same aqua color my bridesmaids wore for my wedding years ago.
- *Nature.* If you are inspired by nature, perhaps you can bring the out-of-doors indoors. Suzann loves flowers. They are found on her wallpaper, in her framed artwork, and collected in vases around her home.
- *Art.* Maybe a certain piece of artwork or a type of faux painting technique inspires you. Arts and crafts can inspire a decorating theme.
- *Objects.* Laurie Smith, a *Trading Spaces* home-decorating designer, suggests that we allow ourselves to be inspired by an object—a rug, a piece of art, a vase, a flower. She encourages women to look for styles, colors, and objects for which we have a passion, and warns us not to buy things just to keep up with trends or fill empty spaces. She writes, "I would rather see a newly married couple have a home sparsely furnished with pieces that mean something to them than a house crammed with furniture they will tire of in ten years."[2] What good advice!

For some, it can be tempting to invest too much time, money, and energy in the pursuit of a beautiful home. You'll create discontentment and anxiety in your husband—and others who come into your home—when perfection is your goal. Remember your purpose for creating a culture of beauty: to love and refresh the people in your life.

Define your individual expression of beauty and go for it—within reason! In that way, the beautiful environment you create will give energy to those in your home.

BEAUTY'S ATTITUDE

A woman can make or break the beautiful environment in her home with her attitude. "The tongue is a small thing, but what enormous damage it can do. A tiny spark can set a great forest on fire" (James 3:5). A woman's tongue can be the spark that sets her home ablaze or builds it up. What does your tongue do?

Promote Peace Instead of Quarreling

When things don't go your way, do you resort to complaining or arguing until things do? Selfishness is often at the root of quarreling. Picture two toddlers arguing over the same toy. "It's mine," they both say. We teach them not to be selfish, yet we do the same thing when we demand our way. Insisting on having it our way yields contention, not the beauty of peace in our homes. People (including husbands) rarely feel comfortable in this environment and will often seek refuge elsewhere.

To create beautiful homes that others enjoy being in, we must pursue peace. Joyce Meyer says, "You have to pursue peace . . . in the same way we pursue relationships, jobs, fun or anything else worthy of our attention and effort. It is something we must choose, and when we do so over and over and over again, we diminish the enemy's influence in our lives, and the door is opened wide to all that God has for us!"[3]

Pursuing peace daily helps us to hear God's voice. It's difficult to hear God's voice when we're stirred up, anxious, or angry—our own voice of protest drowns out the Lord's. He says, "Come to me with your ears wide open. Listen, for the life of your soul is at stake" (Isaiah 55:3). If you want resolution in the midst of a struggle, you'll want to hear God's voice. He's got the answer to your problems.

Romans 12:18 says, "Do your part to live in peace with everyone, as much as possible." This godly attitude of peace brings beauty into our homes.

Cultivate Contentment Instead of Complaining

Is it your habit to complain? Many women make a practice of complaining to their husbands. Nothing seems to be good enough—the way her husband handles money, how little time he spends with the children, how rarely he completes jobs around the house, his lack of a spiritual leadership role within the home—and she can't wait to tell him about it. You've probably heard it before, but refused to admit that it applies to you: "A nagging wife is as annoying as the constant dripping on a rainy day. Trying to stop her complaints is like trying to stop the wind or hold something with greased hands" (Proverbs 27:15–16).

Realistically, can you effect change through complaining and nagging?

The Bible sends a clear message to women: "There are husbands who, indifferent as they are to any words about God, will be captivated by your life of holy beauty" (1 Peter 3:1–2 MSG). Another translation of this verse states that husbands "may be won without a word by the behavior of their wives" (RSV). Complaining breaches the boundary of "without a word"!

If you are dissatisfied with the actions and behavior of your husband, go to God with it. Ask God if the issues, which raise the hair on the back of your neck, are bothering Him. So often, when I take this question to my Heavenly Father, He speaks to me about *me*. There is usually something in me He wants to change. The change He works in you could be the "life of holy beauty" that will captivate your husband. If you are dealing with serious, sinful issues related to your husband, deal with them in a loving way (see chapter 8, "Speaking Truth in Love").

After taking your complaint to God, choose to focus on the positive aspects of your husband. This may be difficult at times, but this will draw your attention back to what you first found attractive in him. When you were dating, he was likely won over by your admiration of him. Get in touch with those golden memories and make them a regular subject of your thoughts.

It may also be tempting for you to complain about other people or problems in your life—your in-laws, your financial situation, perceived slights from friends, and so on. No one has a perfect life, and you must decide what type of attitude you want filling your home. Contentment ushers beauty into the home. When struggling with discontentment, begin thanking God for what He's done for you. Thanksgiving is a special love-language that blesses God and releases blessings of joy into your life. Try it!

In prison, Paul wrote, "I have learned, in whatever state I am, to be content" (Philippians 4:11 RSV). It doesn't matter what you go through—God is your refuge and peace available in any storm. Quiet your noisy tongue. Refuse to dirty your house with complaints and instead create beauty in your home by cultivating contentment.

Strive to Be Slow to Anger Instead of Quick Tempered.

Proverbs 21:19 says it is "better to dwell in the wilderness, than with a contentious and angry woman" (NKJV). The unfortunate fellow who lives with an angry wife has moved out of the house all the way to the desert! Stop, and let this thought sink in: a hot, dry, waterless wilderness is preferable to life with an angry woman. This should be enough to get our attention about taming our tempers.

A quick temper signals trouble from within. Anger's root is pain or fear that you're experiencing today with ties back to unresolved conflicts from the past. These unresolved issues are like sores covered by scabs that fall off when someone accidentally aggravates your wound. It hurts, the wounds are re-exposed, and you cry out in anger.

If you want to create a culture of beauty in your home, it's time to engage in some soul searching. If the fullness of your heart produces angry reactions, ask God to reveal the source of your pain. Psalm 139:23–24 says, "Search me, O God, and know my heart; try me and know my anxieties; and see if there is any wicked way in me, and lead me in the way everlasting" (NKJV).

When I'm quick to anger, I've learned to ask God to reveal what's going on inside me. Why am I lashing out with a sharp tongue? Why am I displeased with everyone? I find that it's rarely others who are the cause of my anger, but rather it's caused by something within me. Sometimes it's simply a matter of needing more rest. At other times, God has revealed to me sin to repent of or hurt in need of healing. Often I'm convicted by the Holy Spirit to forgive someone who has hurt me, or to confess that fear is motivating my angry outbursts. When I remember that God hasn't given me a spirit of fear, I can take my fearful thoughts captive and make them obedient to Christ. Then His power, love, and a sound mind are returned to me.

When you find yourself short-tempered and angry, stop and ask God to reveal the source of what's troubling you. As you draw near to God, He will gently instruct and guide you in the path of righteousness. Listen and obey. This is the path of blessing.

Set the Temperature

Your attitude is the atmospheric gauge in your home. Your positive attitude has the power to raise your family's spirit. Likewise, your negative attitude creates a chill in the air that your whole family senses. How does that phrase go? "If momma ain't happy, ain't nobody happy."

Perhaps you're not the one quarreling, complaining, or angry. Perhaps someone else in your home is exuding these negative attitudes. The good news is: your own happiness depends on the attitude you decide to have. Minister and positive-thinking proponent Norman Vincent Peale said, "Attitudes are more important than facts"! Decide what kind of atmosphere you want to provide for your family and others looking for refuge.

Good attitudes create a culture of beauty in your home.

BEAUTY'S FOCUS

The beauty of the relationships in your home is of far greater value than having a home that could be featured in *Better Homes and Gardens*. A woman desiring to create a culture of beauty will *focus* on the *people* in her home!

"Yes, a woman can and must be involved in the world outside of the home. But first [God] asks us to take very seriously the needs of those who dwell inside our homes."[4] As Proverbs 31:27 says, "She keeps an eye on everyone in her household. . . ." (MSG). As women, we're hardwired to detect relational issues. Above all else, focus on the needs—spiritual, emotional, and physical—represented by the people living in your home.

Focus on Your Husband

Are you focused on creating a beautiful relationship with your husband? I recently received an email containing the following excerpt:

> The busy Bianca is that wife that is always too busy with everything that is not related to her husband. Some wives get so busy with their work and with their children that they end up putting their marriage on hold. How can one be too busy for the most important part of her life? How can your children be happy and fulfilled, if their parents have broken up? How can your work succeed and prosper you, if it makes you rich, but alone? How can your charitable work toward others mean anything, if the ones closest to you are the ones most needy?

Most wives, if asked, would say their relationship with their husband is very important to them. If this is true, our choices will reflect it. Just as with any friendship, the quality of our marriage declines if we spend little time together.

If you have a busy life, you may need to make concessions in order to have a focused relationship with your husband. Pray, and ask God to show you what you could give up in order to have more time to engage in your marriage.

As I've traveled beyond the borders of the United States, I've reflected on the things which commonly distract North Americans from our relationships—things which are not as prevalent in other countries: our drive to acquire possessions, our eagerness to involve our children in as many activities as possible, our heightened appetite for entertainment, and the speed with which we rush from one activity to another. We fill our God-given time with a blur of motion. Are these things worth losing the intimacy we could have if we focused on our relationship with our husband?

As a young mother, I thought I was controlling our family's pace by limiting my children to one extracurricular activity each. With three children at home, this kept me busy and on the run more than I would have liked. Many evenings I returned home exhausted, unable to focus on my husband.

If you think this pattern of busyness will end when your children leave home, you are mistaken. As empty nesters, my husband and I find ourselves with more time and ability to entertain ourselves—many times rushing from one activity to another, flooding our bodies with adrenaline which fuels us to rush more. When we finally arrive home, we're far too tired to focus on one another.

This lack of focus is detrimental to a relationship. The biblical illustration of sowing and reaping found in 2 Corinthians 9, where it is a picture of financial investment in God's work, can be applied to our marital relationship investments. Consider: "He who sows sparingly will also reap sparingly, and he who sows bountifully will also reap bountifully" (verse 6 RSV). If you are sowing all your seed in soil outside your marriage, your marriage will not benefit at harvest time.

You must choose to focus on your marriage before it becomes fruitless and barren. Your fulfillment, the well-being of your husband, and the security of your children are the fruit of that focus.

Focus on Children

How can you bring beauty into your relationship with your children at home? What experiences can you create that will live long in the memory of a child? Focusing on your children doesn't mean putting them first or dropping everything to chauffer them to the latest event. It involves looking at them (not over them), listening to them (the first time), hugging them (lots), and enjoying time spent with them (even helping with homework).

Maybe you and your husband haven't taken the step of parenting yet, first working to accomplish other goals. Or perhaps one or both of you don't think of yourself as "parent material" and have agreed to focus your energies elsewhere. Or maybe you are one of the many wives who long for children but have been unable to conceive. All of my siblings have struggled with infertility and I've watched their pain cut deep. If that's your situation, I grieve with you. Whatever your situation, if you don't have children of your own, would you consider directing the flow of your love toward someone else's child who is not receiving the love he or she needs? Because we live in a fallen world, there are many children lacking a loving parental relationship. Look for opportunities to include others' children in your home. The children of single parents, especially, need lots of extra support, and something as simple as transporting them to church once a week could make an eternal difference in their lives. Even if the children have good relationships with their parents, having another adult pouring beauty into their lives will not be wasted. Jesus cared about children and told us that when we care for children, we care about what's important to Him (Matthew 19:14).

The Beauty of Special Memories. Tom and I enjoy the privilege of spending one night a week with our granddaughters. One of their favorite activities during "Granny and Pa date night" is donning their favorite aprons and helping me make dinner. Once the dinner is made and the table set (with everyone's favorite colored plate) they'll light candles and call Pa down to dinner. They're proud as peacocks when Pa comments on the beautiful table and the delicious food. After dinner, we'll either turn on a favorite CD and dance together, or maybe we'll throw layers of pillows and blankets on the floor and watch a movie. This night is all about focusing on them, doing things they enjoy. They each look forward to it all week long.

When three little girls are at work in my kitchen, the unexpected often happens. Eggshells land in the omelet, lemonade spills on the rug, and the majority of carefully measured spices reach the counter instead of the meatloaf. As a grandparent with the gift of perspective, I relish these opportunities to focus on my relationship with my grandkids rather than protect my clean house.

Think of ways that you can focus on building beautiful memories for your children—bake and decorate gingerbread men, build forts made of blankets, make special traditions, and cook a favorite meal for the birthday child. I realize moms deal with mishaps on a daily basis and are often overwhelmed, as I was when I was raising our kids. I know it can be tempting to meet your need for order before meeting your child's need for making sweet memories. But your home won't feel beautiful when your behavior indicates more concern for your clean house than for your child.

On the other hand, maybe you struggle to keep a neat, orderly home. Chaos and disorder won't feel beautiful or refreshing to your kids (or husband), either. Get a helpful book, or advice from a friend, and take small steps toward creating a more organized home—you'll be glad you did.

The Beauty of the Dinner Table. In my opinion, the beauty of a home is synonymous with family mealtime. Precious family memories are formed around the dinner table. Yet, the number of meals shared together by families has drastically declined over the last several decades.

Why are mealtimes spent together so important? Eating meals together as a family can be one of the best ways to help you establish beautiful relationships and help your children make good choices in life.

WebMD.com cites the following benefits of frequent family dinners, based on statistics from The National Center on Addiction and Substance Abuse at Columbia University:

+ Everyone eats healthier meals.
+ Kids are less likely to become overweight or obese.
+ They're more likely to stay away from cigarettes.
+ They're less likely to drink alcohol.
+ They won't likely try marijuana.
+ They're less likely to use illicit drugs.
+ Their school grades will be better.
+ There will be less stress and tension at home.[5]

Few things are as comforting as a home cooked meal, yet hectic schedules often keep women out of the kitchen. Thankfully, we can continue the traditional mealtime with a little help:

+ Rachael Ray's *Thirty Minute Meals* is one of my favorite television programs. From start to finish, the entire meal takes thirty minutes to prepare. Her cookbook, *Rachael Ray 365: No Repeats*, includes one thirty-minute meal for every day of the year.
+ There are several cookbooks devoted to one-dish slow cooker meals. You could fill your slow cooker in the morning, set it, and let it do the work for you.
+ Prepare meals in advance. In many cities, you can visit a business which helps you prepare a week's or month's worth of meals—they've done all the shopping, and they clean up the mess. Of course, they charge a fee for this service, but it might

be a workable option to ensure you have dinnertime as a family at least once a week.

+ Get together with other women to cook in community once a month. Store your prepared meals in the freezer.
+ Maybe your husband or children have culinary skills! Encourage their involvement—even at the expense of a mess in the kitchen. Make a trade. They cook—you clean.

Here are some tips for making the most of family mealtimes:

+ Involve everyone in preparing the food and setting the table.
+ Shut off the TV, Wii, iPods, iPads, etc. and ignore phones (cell or otherwise), texts, or voice messages.
+ Light candles.
+ Play soft background music.
+ Hold hands during prayer.
+ Allow every family member to share highlights from their day.
+ Have family devotions while everyone is still seated.
+ Share something "interesting" about the Bible passage.
+ Do dishes together afterward.

I can't overemphasize the importance of family mealtime. After all these years, I still love going home to my mom's for dinner and my grown children enjoy coming home for dinner, too.

Focus on Those in Need

When did you last offer hospitality to a guest or stranger? There are many people who could benefit from a warm and friendly dose of hospitality. Romans 12:13 reminds us, "When God's children are in need, be the one to help them out. And get into the habit of inviting guests home for dinner or, if they need lodging, for the night."

There are many hurting people with real needs all around you. Are any of your children's friends from a broken or abusive home and in need of your warmth and generosity? Do you or your husband have a co-worker who is dealing with difficult issues and in need of friendship? Do you know someone without a job who could use a free meal and some encouragement? Invite them into your home and demonstrate care for them.

Years ago when my children were young, after homeschool was finished for the day I'd escape to the garden for some much-needed self-care. A young neighbor girl would often wander into my yard during that time. Sadly, I brushed her off many a time. Today I regret that action as I've seen evidence of her struggles (from afar) throughout her teen years. Though that time set aside for self-care was vital for my well-being, I could have reached out to her at another time by inviting her to dinner occasionally or asking her to join me in pulling weeds. God presents each of us with opportunities to extend hospitality by offering warmth and compassion to those in need. If someone keeps popping into your life uninvited or unexpectedly, consider what God wants you to do for them.

Do you avoid extending hospitality because your home is less than picture-perfect? A picture-perfect home gives the illusion that you don't have struggles—which may cause further despair in someone who does. Your focus shouldn't be the decorating or furniture but rather the one in need of your hospitality.

When Tom and I lived in North Carolina, we were far from home, lonely, and in need of friendship. There was a couple in our church who didn't have many worldly possessions, but one thing they possessed in abundance was hospitality. They frequently invited us over to share what little they had and we developed a friendship.

Throw wide your doors and be on the lookout for those in need of refuge from one of life's storms. A focus on hospitality turns your home into a place of shelter for lost and lonely people.

Create a culture of beauty in your home through your individual expression, godly attitudes, and a focus on your husband, children, and those in need—and may all who enter experience the energy beauty creates.

Reflection

1. What does your home tell of you? Does your home display your personal expression of beauty?

2. What is your personal style of expressing beauty? Romantic, adventurous, serene, or something else? What could you do to begin expressing your individual style?

3. What is the atmosphere like in your home—low or high pressure? Is this due to quarreling, complaining, or anger in which you are involved? If so, journal about what triggers the emotional barometer to rise.

4. What are your husband's positive qualities? Keep a running list in your prayer journal. When you're tempted to complain about something he does, refer back to it to help you focus on the good.

5. What takes your focus from your relationship with your husband, children, or hospitality? What actions can you take to redirect your focus? Journal your ideas.

6. Do you regularly sit down to eat as a family? If not, what steps could you take to make this a priority? Make a list of any obstacles preventing family dinnertime along with solutions for how to overcome them.

First Steps

1. Think about your personal expression of beauty and add a touch of it to your favorite room.

2. Share a plan with your husband for expressing your personal style at home and discuss a budget for any changes you'd like to make. Explore the possibility of selling some

things that don't express your uniqueness (with your husband's consent) in order to purchase others.

3. Eliminate one thing or activity that distracts you from your relationship with your husband.
4. Eat dinner—preferably homecooked, but carryout works too—with your family at the dinner table.
5. Confess any negative attitudes that have plagued you and ask your husband to pray for you as you begin replacing them with godly attitudes.
6. In your prayer journal, make a list of hurting, struggling people (adults or children) who might benefit from some warm hospitality in your home. Share the list with your husband and ask for names of people he may want to invite (maybe someone at work). Plan now to begin inviting them one by one.

CHAPTER ELEVEN

Professionalizing the Roles of Wife and Mother

*Her children stand and bless her. Her husband praises
her: "There are many virtuous and capable women in
the world, but you surpass them all!"*
—PROVERBS 31:28–29

*Let's admit that family life tries us as perhaps nothing
else does; but let's also accept that, for most of us, this is
God's call and part of his plan to perfect us.*
—GARY THOMAS, *SACRED PARENTING*

*F*ew consider the role of wife or mother to be as serious a profession as they would business, education, or law. But the
truth is that a woman who chooses to become a wife and mother has
embarked upon two of the most challenging and important careers
there are—careers that often produce more questions than answers,
more guilt than peace, and more longings than contentment. However, professionalizing these roles gives women the opportunity to
grow and be blessed in unexpected ways.

Author Gary Thomas writes:

Let's accept that both marriage and parenting provide many
good moments while also challenging us to the very root of our

199

being. . . . It becomes a sacred enterprise when we finally understand that God can baptize dirty diapers, toddlers' tantrums, and teenagers' silence in order to transform us into people who more closely resemble Jesus Christ.[1]

In any profession, you lay the groundwork for success by developing a strategic career plan. This strategic plan includes talking to your boss, creating a vision and corresponding plan of action, getting education, and listening to good mentors.

THE PROFESSIONAL WIFE'S STRATEGY FOR SUCCESS

Talk to Your Boss

You live in a broken world. This means that, throughout the life of your marriage, situations will leave you feeling brokenhearted, lonely, or confused. You'll feel at a loss as to what is expected of you. At times like these, talk to your Boss! God is waiting for you to come and talk to Him. He wants to hold you in His arms of love, listen to every word you say, and comfort you. As you pray and read His Word, He'll give you the wisdom you seek. There isn't anything you'll face that He can't handle.

Tom and I have been married since 1980, and we still encounter times of difficulty. Every marriage does. I often need to talk to God so I can receive comfort, wisdom, and grace to proceed.

Some of the problems I experience are made more complicated when I try to handle them on my own before talking to God. When I talk to Him, His comfort and guidance fills me with unexpected peace. When I follow His counsel, the events of my life turn out better than I imagined.

At other times, the answers I need don't come quickly or easily. During times of prolonged suffering, you have an opportunity to cling more tightly to Jesus and receive more of His power made perfect in your weakness. His power will revive and strengthen you—

enabling you to do what He asks and wait patiently for prayers to be answered. Talk to God. There is no condemnation awaiting you, only help and hope in time of need.

Determine a Vision for Your Role as a Wife

"Vision energizes life. It inspires. It clarifies. It harnesses the powers and abilities of one's life and focuses them on a prescribed end."[2]

When I got married, I didn't have a vision for my role as a wife. I was nineteen, pregnant, and very immature. My thoughts centered around the fanciful hope that everything would work out fine for Tom and me despite the fact that our engagement had been characterized by anger, selfishness, and manipulation. From day one, our marriage was distinguished by emotional abuse. Instead of determining a vision, I dabbled in wishful thinking, imagining that our problems would simply work themselves out.

God used the difficulty in my life to grow me up in Him. It took me awhile, but a vision for how God wanted to use me within my marriage began forming in my heart as a result of godly mentoring, Christian counseling, and discovering the truth of God's Word for myself. Clinging to the vision He inspired within me, I was preserved from drowning in my problems and becoming one more failed marriage statistic.

The vision that God inspired within me for the benefit of my marriage included speaking truth in love (Ephesians 4:15), growing in compassion (Ephesians 4:32), and becoming a woman of strength and dignity (Proverbs 31:25). These were values God wanted to develop in me for the good of my marriage.

The vision God has for you may become clearer when you consider your personal weaknesses that God wants to strengthen for the good of your marriage. God may also inspire a vision based on strengths He's gifted you with that He wants to use to bless your husband. Be careful here: Don't come on too strong! Approaching your husband with humility and respect will be key when developing your plan of action.

Also consider the areas in which your husband struggles. The emotional abuse I was experiencing was a significant clue as to how God wanted to use me in my marriage. He was calling on me to speak truth in love to my husband.

Though my vision was birthed from a position of desperation (and yours may be too), others of you can pray for an inspired vision from a better place. Either way, vision is critical to the strength of your marriage.

Proverbs 29:18 (AMP) speaks to the importance of vision: "Where there is no vision [no redemptive revelation of God], the people perish." A vision keeps you from a life of self-defeat. Robert Lewis writes, "A life that is not called forward will stagnate or fall backward into trouble. Life becomes aimless, twisted, and disoriented. Without vision people naturally tend to wander. Bad decisions follow."[3]

When determining a vision, choose values that are within your power to control. A joint vision for your marriage is wonderful but dependent on your husband's buy-in. If you try to establish a joint vision that's representative of your union, and he doesn't choose to join you, you'll experience discouragement. Being equipped with a personal vision will harness your own powers and abilities, bring strength to your marriage, and bless your husband.

Ask God to inspire a vision within you. God knows the needs of your marriage and how you can best meet these needs as a wife. He will give you the wisdom you need if you'll only ask.

Once God inspires you with a vision, *write it down* in a journal. Writing your vision helps you remember it. As you stay focused on your vision, you'll be motivated to make choices that will bring it to pass.

Develop a Plan of Action

When your vision is written down, it's time to develop a plan of action in your journal. What steps could you take today, this month, or this year to draw nearer to your vision? You may have already identified some steps, perhaps through the First Steps listed at the conclusion of each chapter in this book. If not, God will guide you to a step-by-step plan of action as you seek education and mentoring.

Get an Education

Decide what education you need to move forward with your vision. For instance, if your vision includes mutual respect in your marriage, but you have trouble respecting your husband, you could read *Love and Respect* by Emerson Eggerichs and study what the Bible says about respect.

If you want compassion to be a hallmark of your life, study Jesus' love and compassion for you as seen in the Gospels. Watch compassionate people. Serve those less fortunate. When God inspired my vision to focus on speaking the truth in love, I had to study and learn how to do that. I read books on the subject and collected Bible verses that encouraged me in this area. With the help of a Christian counselor, I dealt with the fears that kept me silent when I should have spoken up for Tom's and my benefit.

Find Scripture verses that will support your pursuit of the vision God has set before you. List them in a journal. Meditate on them. Memorize them, hiding them in your heart to keep you from becoming stagnant or falling backward into trouble.

Find a Mentor

Another important step toward realizing your vision is identifying those who can help you. Along with talking to God, godly women and mentors will help you move toward the good things you envision for your marriage.

God has used other women to help cheer me along my journey of marriage. You need this, too. Make a list of women who you think will encourage you to be a woman of God who presses toward the call of her vision. Ask them if they will be willing to encourage and hold you accountable to your plan of action. You will be strengthened in a community of women.

Whether your marriage is currently flourishing or struggling, implementing a strategic plan will help you. If your marriage is in a good place, take this time to pour your efforts into your strategic plan. Hone your skills; add new ones. Make it a habit to grow your marriage. Once it's a habit, you will be well prepared when difficult times come. If you're in a tough place, developing and following a strategic plan will help you chart a course forward.

Realistically, every marriage encounters its own unique brand of struggles. Whether you face difficulties concerning finances, health, infertility, children, or immorality, this strategy for success will reward you with increased peace, joy, and fulfillment in your career as a professional wife.

THE PROFESSIONAL MOTHER'S STRATEGY FOR SUCCESS

If you're already a mother or if you hope to mother someday, this section is for you. G. K. Chesterton said that a mother of a young child is "with a human being at a time when he asks all the questions that there are, and some that there aren't." Chesterton appreciated the magnitude of the demands on a mother! "How can it be a large career to tell other people's children about the Rule of Three [in other words, be a teacher], and a small career to tell one's own children about the universe?" he asks. The obvious answer is, *it's not!* "A woman's function is laborious," he concludes, "because it is gigantic, not because it is minute!"[4] And without a strategy for success, you'll be ill-equipped for this gigantic role.

Establish Unity with Your Colleague

Ultimately, if you have a spouse and children, the roles of professional wife and professional mother are intricately linked. The health of your marriage has great impact on the lives of your children. Focus on achieving unity with your husband, and your parenting efforts will be blessed.

Psalm 133 says, "How wonderful it is, how pleasant, when brothers live together in harmony! For harmony is as precious as the fragrant anointing oil that was poured over Aaron's head, that ran down his beard and onto the border of his robe. Harmony is as refreshing as the dew from Mount Hermon that falls on the mountains of Zion. And the LORD has pronounced his blessing, even life forevermore."

What does all this mean when talking about parenting children? First, it tells us that unity is good and pleasant for those who possess it. Harmonious relationships make us all happy.

Second, unity is like precious oil that releases a wonderful fragrance and extends downward toward your children. When you and your husband are on the same page, your children will experience more peace and less stress and confusion.

Third, unity "cools the scorching heat of men's passions, as the evening dews cool the air and refresh the earth. It contributes very much to our fruitfulness in every thing that is good, it moistens the heart, and makes it tender and fit to receive the good seed of the word."[5] Unity between you and your husband aids your children in growing strong in the things of God. The harmony of your marriage is critical to the growth of every godly character trait you wish to instill in the hearts of your children.

Fourth, the proof of unity can be seen in the blessings that accompany it. God sees to it that those who dwell unified are blessed.

Mutual Respect. With all the blessings unity provides, why don't more marriages experience it? Unity thrives on respect. It's easier to listen to or trust your husband's opinion when you feel that he respects what you're doing. It's difficult to achieve unity with your husband if he doesn't respect your work as a mom. The following email illustrates the frustration that occurs when a man doesn't respect the work of a mom.

WHAT DO YOU DO ALL DAY?

A man came home from work and found his three children outside, still in their pajamas, playing in the mud, with empty food boxes and wrappers strewn all around the front yard.

The door of his wife's car was open, as was the front door to the house and there was no sign of the dog.

Proceeding into the entry, he found an even bigger mess. A lamp had been knocked over, and the throw rug was wadded against one wall.

In the front room the TV was loudly blaring a cartoon channel, and the family room was strewn with toys and various items of clothing.

In the kitchen, dishes filled the sink, breakfast food was spilled on the counter, the fridge door was open wide, dog food was spilled on the floor, a broken glass lay under the table, and a small pile of sand was spread by the back door.

He quickly headed up the stairs, stepping over toys and more piles of clothes, looking for his wife. He was worried she might be ill, or that something serious had happened.

He was met with a small trickle of water as it made its way out the bathroom door. As he peered inside he found wet towels, scummy soap, and more toys strewn over the floor. Miles of toilet paper lay in a heap and toothpaste had been smeared over the mirror and walls.

As he rushed to the bedroom, he found his wife still curled up in bed in her pajamas, reading a novel. She looked up at him, smiled, and asked how his day went. He looked at her bewildered and asked, "What happened here today?"

She again smiled and answered, "You know every day when you come home from work and you ask me what in the world I do all day?"

"Yes," was his incredulous reply.

She answered, "Well, today I didn't do it."

Whether you are a stay-at-home or a working mom, if your husband doesn't respect the magnitude of all you do throughout the day—it hurts. Mothers do more than anyone notices.

The important thing to remember is that God has called you to this gigantic job. You are working for Him. He calls mothers to a job He highly respects—serving the vulnerable. When you love and care for your children, He notices and is very pleased! Recognize your job as the most important there is. Then, when you come to the table of unity, you can listen with an open mind to your husband's opinions with the knowledge that God values yours as well.

It may be helpful to communicate with your husband about all you are doing. As impossible as it may seem—he may not realize everything you do. Perhaps he needs your prayers before he will understand the importance of the role a mother fills.

Resolving Differences. Unity can also be illusive if you and your husband come into marriage with different ideas about parenting. There are exceptions, but typically you'll parent as you were parented.

You and your husband must talk about this important issue and come to a consensus about how you will parent in unity. Maintaining unity depends on all you have learned as a professional wife. Sometimes you'll need to speak up for your beliefs (Assertiveness—"Speaking Truth in Love"), and sometimes you will need to yield to your husband (Respect—"Inviting Romance").

When you or your husband raises a red flag concerning decisions regarding your children, how should you proceed? God will confirm His direction for you through one or more of the following ways:[6]

- Holy Spirit. The Holy Spirit alerts you to specific answers to specific questions through listening prayer and insight from Scripture. Pray together regarding your children and ask the Holy Spirit to guide you.
- Common sense and God's wisdom. Both you and your husband can tap into your combined reservoir of common sense

when parenting your children. Balancing common sense with biblical principles helps confirm God's direction. The book of Proverbs is loaded with parenting advice.

+ Signs and circumstances. You or your husband may read something that points to an answer, or stumble across something that seems like a sign, or hear a sermon that is a word from the Lord directly to you regarding the issue you are facing with your children. However, if you are looking for signs or circumstances to confirm what you want to do, it might not be God. It's easy to find justification for what you want, so it is wise to balance signs or circumstances with additional confirmation.

+ Wise counsel. The book of Proverbs tells us that plans fail for lack of counsel (15:22). You can often confirm God's direction when you seek wise counsel from people you trust.

+ Supernatural guidance. God can guide you through dreams, or by giving you a word through someone who doesn't even know the situation that you and your husband are facing.

When you and your husband disagree, wait. Don't proceed until you've come into unity. Although this is hard work, you will be blessed for your faithfulness. "The process of parenting is one of the most spiritually formative journeys a man and a woman can ever undertake. . . . The journey of caring for, raising, training, and loving children will mark us indelibly and powerfully. We cannot be the same people we once were; we will be forever changed, eternally altered."[7] Establishing unity with your husband will bring spiritual rewards in your marriage as well as your career as a professional mother.

Talk to Your Boss

As a professional mother, you run up against problems on a daily basis for which you'll need help. If you ask and wait for God's help, you'll receive it.

As a mother of three children, I regularly talked to God about the problems I experienced. Unfortunately, after I brought my troubles to Him, I often left before listening to His advice. I believed that through the act of prayer, God was going to rescue me and change everything. However, God doesn't release you from your responsibility or magically change things simply because you're talking to Him. You are your child's mother and God wants to help you by working through *you*.

Once you've shared your problem with God—wait. That's right, be still. He will guide you if you quiet yourself and listen. Listening to God by being quiet, reading the Word, and listening to godly mentors adds wisdom to your parenting.

As I talk to God about my adult children and the problems they face, I've learned to wait for His guidance. Most often, He speaks to me about *me* when I'm quiet or reading the Bible. He's maturing me not only for my sake, but also for the sake of my children. Now, I more clearly reflect my Savior's love for my children—a love which holds the power to heal all those who come in contact with it. One way God works in the lives of my adult children is through my changed actions! God wants to work in the life of your child through your changed life. Whatever your child's age, begin now to listen to God's wisdom for you and your parenting. Your children will notice the change as mine have.

Ben Carson's mom talked to God about her problem. A poor, single mother of two young boys, she prayed that God would give her wisdom for her son who was a failing student. She waited, listened, and found guidance to limit her son's television watching to three shows a week. During the time he would normally watch television, he instead would read two books and give his mother written reports on them. "This was the beginning of a change that set young Ben's life on a new course. . . . [He] went on to become one of the world's most sought-after pediatric neurosurgeons, known for his creativity."[8]

If you see trouble brewing in the life of your child, don't ignore it. Maybe you're too busy to observe negative behavior in your child. Maybe you're justifying or rationalizing the problems you see. Maybe you don't have the energy to "go there." These are dangerous choices.

If you don't deal with these issues now, they will grow and harm your child. For the sake of your child, lay aside distractions and pray—listen for the instruction that will come.

God is a never-ending source of wisdom for all your parenting problems.

Determine a Vision Concerning Your Children

As in marriage, it is important to have a vision for all you hope to accomplish as a mother in the lives of your children. It is a great responsibility to raise the next generation. If you have a vision, it will motivate you to work toward the good things you desire for your children.

It's difficult for a mother without vision to stay on the course that God has for her and her children. The culture's strong current pulls many children away from the good things their parents want for them; this is not a time to float aimlessly. Did you know Satan has a vision for your children? He wants to see them destroyed. "The Devil. . . . prowls around like a roaring lion, looking for some victim to devour" (1 Peter 5:8). A professional mother with a clear vision for her children is proactively protecting her children from Satan's evil schemes.

What vision has God placed in your heart for your kids? What character qualities do you want to see in them when they're five, ten, thirteen, and seventeen years old? Make sure these qualities are first something God has developed in your own life and then set your course, hoist your sails, and aim for a godly vision.

As a professional mother, you have been given responsibility for the lives of your children. No matter what their ages, start now to make a strategic plan for success. Determine the vision God has for them and write it down in your prayer journal!

Develop a Plan of Action

Once your vision is clear, develop an action plan that will lead you to the vision God has given you.

Angie wants to hide God's Word in her children's hearts because she's seen its power at work in her own life, so she prays the Word over them every morning. She knows there are some verses they can quote easily because they hear her say them every day. With her vision in place, she's developed a plan of action that is bearing fruit.

As a Christian mother, the salvation of each child should be at the top of your vision list. Developing a plan of action will articulate how you can aid the process of your child receiving Christ as their Lord and Savior. Talk with them about the power of salvation in your own life. Engage in an evangelistic ministry as a family. During family devotions, choose verses that motivated you to recognize your need for Christ.

According to your vision, what action steps can you take to proceed in the right direction? Record them in your prayer journal.

Get an Education

Because your children will model themselves after what they see in your life more than what you teach them, you must educate yourself in any area that you are weak. If you lack the skills you want them to emulate—get an education! Filling your mind and heart with the good things an education provides will produce an overflow into the minds and hearts of your children.

Deuteronomy 6:6–7 (MSG) says, "Write these commandments that I've given you today on your hearts. Get them inside of you and then get them inside your children. Talk about them wherever you are, sitting at home or walking in the street; talk about them from the time you get up in the morning to when you fall into bed at night." Until you have been educated, you'll be unable to play a vital role in establishing the vision you have for your children. What must you learn first before you can model it to your children?

If you want your children to love unconditionally, you'll need to love them unconditionally first. If you have trouble loving this way, then you don't fully understand the forgiveness you've received through salvation. Educate yourself: read the Bible. Search for verses that talk about how God loved you and died for you when you were still sinning. Memorize them. Think about them. The more you understand God's love, the more you'll be motivated to love your children unconditionally.

If you want your child to forgive others but you struggle to forgive, it will be difficult for your child to learn forgiveness from you. Jesus' model of forgiveness can teach you much. Study Him. Dwell on His words about forgiveness. He forgave you—you can forgive others. Read Christian books on forgiveness such as *Total Forgiveness* by R. T. Kendall. Find a Christian you admire and ask her your questions about forgiveness.

As you begin forgiving your husband and children and others who hurt you, you will be a mirror to your children of God's forgiveness. By humbling yourself through the act of forgiveness, you will pave the way for your children to receive the precious gift of forgiveness for their sins so they will be saved and spend eternity with Christ in heaven.

Maybe your vision includes strengthening your children to weather the storms of life. If you've not learned what to do in the day of adversity, how will you prepare your kids? Start by reading books on trusting God in adversity such as *Turn My Mourning into Dancing* by Henri Nouwen. Talk with other Christians about how they stand firm when life is bleak. Find verses in the Bible about trusting God, and study the men and women in the Bible who stayed loyal to God in evil times.

Practice what you learn. When you go through tough times with a determination to trust God—with His peace clearly evident in your life—you will be teaching your children that it is possible to go through difficult times with God's help. Because so many quit in the midst of adversity, your determination to press through will be a powerful witness to your children.

Are you challenged by a particular struggle with one of your children, such as a learning disability, eating disorder, or ADHD? Become an expert in that area. When you educate yourself about it you will be equipped to initiate a plan of action for fulfilling the vision you have for your children.

Find a Mentor

Younger mothers can learn much from being mentored by other more experienced mothers. Talking together about the situations you face is a helpful and fun way to gain guidance and encouragement for this important career.

It's not only a good idea, it's a God idea. Paul wrote to Titus about the importance of women mentoring women in the art of loving children. "These older women must train the younger women to love their husbands and their children" (Titus 2:4).

Organizations such as MOPS (Mothers of Preschoolers, www .mops.org) provide mothering support, personal growth, and spiritual hope, all to help you be the best mom possible. Moms In Touch (www.momsintouch.org) gathers mothers together to pray for their children and schools. Many churches have weekly Bible studies for moms of young children, and childcare is often provided. Check to see what's available in your area and get involved!

You can find encouragement, help, and support for raising children when you talk with a mentor and learn from her experiences.

In no other role does a woman find herself as vulnerable as in the role of mother. Though you may struggle in your relationship with your husband, few will know it unless you disclose the particulars. On the other hand, your children's antics, attitudes, and aptitudes are on display for the world to see and judge. As a result, you may experience an increased sensitivity to your reputation as a mother.

Jesus didn't concern Himself with protecting His reputation. Though some judged Him unjustly—He was perfect, and they complained—Jesus cared more for us than He did for His reputation. Nowhere is this more evident than at the cross—He was willing to let the whole world think He was a fake whose end had come, so that He could pay for our sins with His death.

This is an example for you, a professional mother, to follow. Your identity as a daughter of God enables you to walk where He leads with the confidence that He is with you. The inner confidence that comes from knowing you're loved by God will produce in you the boldness to face the struggles you encounter in your children's lives. If you are focused on loving and protecting your children, your inclination to worry about your reputation and what others think will lessen.

Your roles as wife and mother are profoundly beautiful. You shape the lives of your husband, children, and generations to come. Can there be any doubt that the roles of a wife and a mother require as much skill—or more—than those required by other professions? This is indeed a profession to be taken seriously! The wife and mother who invests herself fully will reap great rewards, bless her family, and leave a powerful legacy.

Reflection

1. Think of a time when you talked to God concerning a problem in your marriage. Did you wait for God to give you direction? What was the result?
2. In which area as a wife or mother do you lack knowledge and need more education?
3. What benefits might you expect to receive from accountability partners regarding your role as wife? What fears would you need to overcome to make yourself accountable?
4. What obstacle blocks the unity between you and your husband? What steps are you willing to take toward unity?
5. Have you ever determined a vision for your marriage or your children? If not, what do you think kept you from seeing the need to do so? If so, how did you determine this vision?

First Steps

1. With God's help, determine a vision and write it down in your journal. Then develop and journal a plan of action for that vision that will lead to its fulfillment.
   a. For your role as a wife
   b. For your children
2. Present a request for prayer to a Christian mentor or a group of godly friends concerning a weakness in your life that needs strengthening for the sake of your husband and/or your children. Record your request in your prayer journal.
3. Talk with your husband about the benefits of unity in regard to marriage and parenting. Identify which areas you are prone to disagree about. Together, decide on and write down a plan to achieve unity in all decisions, including those affecting your children. Your plan may begin like this: "When we disagree about an issue, we will _____ and _____ in order to reach a unified decision."

CHAPTER TWELVE

Choosing God's Best

Today I have given you the choice between life and death,
between blessings and curses. . . . Oh, that you would
choose life, that you and your descendants might live!
—DEUTERONOMY 30:19

The unpleasant truth [is] that life presents a series of choices,
each of which precludes a host of other attractive possibilities.
—CAITLIN FLANAGAN, "How Serfdom Saved the
Women's Movement," *The Atlantic* (March 2004)

We've plowed a lot of ground over the last eleven chapters, and now that the dust has settled (or has it?), it all comes down to this: choices, choices, choices! A woman has many choices to make that affect her marriage's health. Will you choose trust or control? Budgeting or overspending? A healthy sex life or overcommitment?

The world is quick to proclaim that you don't have to choose: "You can have it all! You can have a great marriage *and* control your husband, financial security by way of materialism, plus run all day *and* have great sex at night." If only the world proclaimed as loudly the desperate stories of women who have tried to cash in on the world's invitation to "have it all" and have failed:

My question is, Who's teaching young women that they can't have it all? The truth is, virtually no one. And when someone like [Maria] Shriver or [Meredith] Vieira ventures out to admit that having it all is a myth, she is usually skewered and quickly dispensed with by so-called progressives who hold that "having it all" is the Holy Grail for women.[1]

Every woman must choose what kind of wife she will be, or she chooses by default. We've all been given the responsibility to choose—beginning with Eve.

Eve wanted more than she had. Perfection wasn't enough! Enticed by the serpent's offer to "become just like God, knowing everything, both good and evil" (Genesis 3:5), she ignored God and traded life for death. Imagine her regret and shame when she realized she'd traded in a full life to get a handful of nothing: separation from God, painful childbirth, and a never-ending power struggle with Adam.

It was a costly choice.

The serpent is still with us today, and he's spewing the same lie Eve believed. Culture agrees with him: "You don't have to choose; you can have everything you want. Never mind that it didn't work for Eve, Maria, or Meredith—it will work for you!" Evidently, women throughout the generations have had the word *gullible* written across their foreheads, for most of us have tried to "have it all" in one way or another.

Make no mistake: you will have to choose. You can't have it all.

WHAT IS THE CHOICE?

Okay, you know you have to choose, but what exactly is the choice? You must choose between your good ideas, desires, and plans, and God's best. Who will govern your decisions: you or God? You're incapable of choosing God's best on your own. Like King David, you need to cry, "Show me the path where I should walk, O LORD; point out the right road for me to follow. Lead me by your truth and teach me, for you are the God who saves me. All day long I put my hope in you" (Psalm 25:4–5).

If you desire to choose God's best, thereby avoiding the pain resulting from sinful choices, you must become humble and obedient.

"He leads the humble in what is right, teaching them his way. The LORD leads with unfailing love and faithfulness all those who keep his covenant and obey his decrees" (Psalm 25:9–10). God's best for your life is found within the boundaries of humility-inspired obedience.

Humility

Like me, you may have discovered that your efforts to grow your relationship with your husband aren't enough. Humbling, isn't it? Maybe you're still in denial, but eventually every woman comes to the same conclusion: I can't do it on my own!

The sooner you let go of pride, the sooner God will take your hand and lead you to His best for your marriage. "He leads the humble in what is right, teaching them his way" (Psalm 25:9).

Humble yourself, and put God on the throne of your life and choices.

Obedience

Obedience produces blessing in your life and marriage! Just as you reward obedient children, so does God. You won't experience God's best if you're disobedient. He won't reward disobedient behavior that is harmful to you or your husband. What kind of Father would He be if He did?

How long will you punish yourself with your own disobedience? There's a better way. Many, including myself, have discovered that "the LORD leads with unfailing love and faithfulness all those who keep his covenant and obey his decrees" (Psalm 25:10).

You know what to do. In the past eleven chapters, you've learned all about your role as you've turned to God and shared within a community of women. Now it's time to obey.

WHERE DO YOU BEGIN?

"You are here!" I love reading those words on maps at roadside parks with big red arrows pointing to my exact location. When I find myself in unfamiliar territory, it's helpful to see where I am in the big picture. I look to those big red arrows when seeking direction for my journey.

Where are you in your journey as a wife? Have you discovered a chapter within this book that pointed to an area in your marriage needing improvement? Does the big red arrow point to diminished romance, a lack of mystique, a habit of overspending, an out-of-control schedule, or a disintegrating sex life? Look closely and be honest. Where are you really? This is the place to target your attention.

For example, my big red arrow points to money mismanagement, so here I go, revisiting the "Managing Money" chapter. Again, I'll ask myself each question in the reflection section and give serious thought to my answers. I'll continue journalling about my attitudes concerning money. I'll live by a predetermined cash spending plan! I'll read books from the recommended reading list in the appendix—checking them out of the library for free, instead of buying them. And I'll pray and ask God to help me obey godly financial principles.

Once I've obeyed God with managing my money, I'll look on the map for the next red arrow—where am I now?—and I'll keep identifying God's truth and obeying it. I'll never stop this process, for my own sake as well as for the sake of my marriage.

No matter where the big red arrow points on your marriage map, humble yourself and obey.

For those times in which you don't choose God's best, there is grace and forgiveness. Repent of your sin to God and forgive yourself—He already has. Allow God and godly mentors to encourage you to step back on the path of His blessing so you won't continue to miss out on His best.

When you begin to experience more and more of God's best for your marriage, consider serving God as a couple. Ministering to those in need not only fulfills God's command to love your neighbor as yourself, but also draws you closer together.

Recently, I had the privilege of serving lunch at a local soup kitchen with my husband and our small group from church. Tom had already made friends with the staff as he had recently become a weekly volunteer. Standing within a few feet of each other, I had a good vantage point from which to observe my husband interacting with those across the counter from him. As Tom carefully placed dessert on each plate, he successfully engaged many patrons in conversation and had a few laughing at his jokes. My heart was warmed watching my husband's tenderness and care for those less fortunate. Together we experienced something holy—something bigger than ourselves—and it drew us together.

Choosing God's best is a continual process you'll repeat again and again in a variety of situations. It's all part of your journey as a wife.

Speaking of the journey, this is where you and I part ways. But I pray this is only the beginning of your pursuit to understand your role as a wife by turning to God and sharing within a community of women. God intended you to be helped, inspired, and encouraged in this way. When women share with each other the details of their journeys with God, it's a beautiful thing indeed.

Reflection

1. In what ways have you tried to "have it all"? How has this affected your marriage? Record these thoughts in your journal.

2. When have you recently tried to improve your marriage or husband without God's help or input? What was the outcome?

3. When have you recently consulted God through His Word and/or godly mentors to guide you in a specific area of your marriage? What was the result?

4. Where does the big red arrow point in your marriage? Write it down. What steps are you willing to take to begin (or continue) choosing God's best in this area? Journal your response.

First Steps

1. Make a plan to meet (or continue to meet) regularly with a loving, honest community of Christian women—sharing the details of your journey with God regarding your role as a wife. Let your husband know your desire to grow as a wife by regularly meeting with other women. Ask for his support.

2. Have you ignored all the journaling prompts in this book? If so, it's possible that you haven't internalized and personalized all that God has for you in your marriage. Try reading the book again, and this time, journal as you go and listen for God's voice.

3. Have you been journaling your way through this book? Keep journaling! It sharpens an understanding of your weaknesses and need for God. Your journal is a place to chronicle all you learn and to be encouraged by God's faithfulness to you. You can refer to your journal(s) throughout your marriage as a go-to source of marital wisdom.

What's Next?

Did this book bless your life and marriage? If so, I encourage you to:

- Share what you've learned with a friend and ask her to hold you accountable.
- Share your comments or testimony with me at www.beautiful womanhood.com.
- Give this book as a gift or wedding present to friends or family members.
- Talk to your women's ministry leader about starting Beautiful Womanhood small groups in your church.
- Pick up *The Beautiful Wife Mentor's Guide* and use this book in a women's Bible study.
- Invite me to speak at a women's event or marriage retreat.
- Link to www.beautifulwomanhood.com from your blog or website.
- Start a discussion about Beautiful Womanhood on Facebook or your favorite social media site.
- Visit www.beautifulwomanhood.com/blog for ongoing Christian marriage encouragement, recommended resources, and advice.

And keep growing as a Christian wife!

Resources for Continued Growth

Equipping for the Journey

Omartian, Stormie. *The Power of a Praying® Wife*. Eugene, OR: Harvest House, 2007.

Thomas, Gary. *Sacred Influence: What a Man Needs from His Wife to Be the Husband She Wants*. Grand Rapids: Zondervan, 2006.

Young, Sarah. *Jesus Calling: Enjoying Peace in His Presence*. Nashville: Thomas Nelson, 2004.

Attending to Self-Care

Colbert, Don. *The Seven Pillars of Health*. Lake Mary, FL: Siloam, 2007.

Peeke, Pamela. *Body for Life for Women: A Woman's Plan for Physical and Mental Transformation*. New York: Rodale, 2005.

Rothschild, Jennifer. *Self Talk, Soul Talk: What to Say When You Talk to Yourself*. Eugene, OR: Harvest House, 2007.

Living as the Genuine Article

Geegh, Mary. *God Guides*. Wausau, WI: Samuel and Lois Geegh and Marcy Geegh Zastrow, 2004.

Slattery, Julianna. *Beyond the Masquerade: Unveiling the Authentic You*. Carol Stream, IL: Tyndale, 2007.

Young, William P. *The Shack: Where Tragedy Confronts Eternity*. Newbury Park, CA: Windblown Media, 2007.

Cultivating Mystique

Eldredge, John, and Stasi Eldredge. *Captivating: Unveiling the Mystery of a Woman's Soul.* Nashville: Thomas Nelson, 2005.

Feldhahn, Shaunti. *The Life Ready Woman: Thriving in a Do-It-All World.* Nashville: B&H, 2011.

Freedom in Christ Ministries. "Who I Am in Christ." http://www.ficm.org/index.php?command=whoamiinchrist.

Heim, Gary, and Lisa Heim. *True North: Choosing God in the Frustrations of Life.* Grand Rapids: Kregel, 2011.

Stafford, Nancy. *Beauty by the Book: Seeing Yourself as God Sees You.* Sisters, OR: Multnomah, 2002.

Welch, Edward T. *When People Are Big and God Is Small: Overcoming Peer Pressure, Codependency, and the Fear of Man.* Resources for Changing Lives. Phillipsburg, NJ: P&R, 1997.

Inviting Romance

Eggerichs, Emerson. *Love & Respect: The Love She Most Desires; The Respect He Desperately Needs.* Nashville: Thomas Nelson, 2004.

Eldredge, John. *Wild at Heart: Discovering the Secret of a Man's Soul.* Rev. exp. ed. Nashville: Thomas Nelson, 2011.

Lipp, Kathi. *The Husband Project: 21 Days of Loving Your Man—on Purpose and with a Plan.* Eugene, OR: Harvest House, 2009.

Schlessinger, Laura. *The Proper Care and Feeding of Husbands.* New York: Harper Paperbacks, 2006.

Thinking Differently About Sex

Cutrer, William, and Sandra Glahn. *Sexual Intimacy in Marriage.* 3rd ed. Grand Rapids: Kregel, 2007.

Dillow, Linda, and Lorraine Pintus. *Intimate Issues: 21 Questions Christian Women Ask About Sex.* Colorado Springs: WaterBrook Press, 1999.

Feldhahn, Shaunti. *For Women Only: What You Need to Know About the Inner Lives of Men.* Sisters, OR: Multnomah, 2004.

Gregoire, Sheila Wray. *Honey, I Don't Have a Headache Tonight: Help for Women Who Want to Feel More "In the Mood."* Grand Rapids: Kregel, 2004.

Leman, Kevin. *Sheet Music: Uncovering the Secrets of Sexual Intimacy in Marriage.* Carol Stream, IL: Tyndale, 2003.

Open Hearts Ministry (www.ohmin.org). *The Journey Begins.* Kalamazoo, MI, 2011.

Rinehart, Paula. *Sex and the Soul of a Woman: The Reality of Love & Romance in an Age of Casual Sex.* Grand Rapids: Zondervan, 2004.

Opening Lines of Communication

Chapman, Gary D. *Now You're Speaking My Language: Honest Communication and Deeper Intimacy for a Stronger Marriage.* Nashville: B&H, 2007.

Eggerichs, Emerson. *Cracking the Communication Code: The Secret to Speaking Your Mate's Language.* Nashville: Thomas Nelson, 2007.

Stanley, Scott, Daniel Trathen, Savanna McCain, and Milt Bryan. *A Lasting Promise: A Christian Guide to Fighting for Your Marriage.* San Francisco: Jossey-Bass, 2002.

Speaking Truth in Love

Cloud, Henry, and John Townsend. *Boundaries in Marriage.* Grand Rapids: Zondervan, 2002.

Hurnard, Hannah. *Hinds' Feet on High Places.* Available in various editions from various publishers.

Koch, Ruth N., and Kenneth C. Haugk. *Speaking the Truth in Love: How to Be an Assertive Christian.* Underlining ed. St. Louis: Stephen Ministries, 1992.

Lucado, Max. *A Love Worth Giving: Living in the Overflow of God's Love.* Nashville: Thomas Nelson, 2002.

Thomas, Gary. *Sacred Marriage: What If God Designed Marriage to Make Us Holy More Than to Make Us Happy?* Grand Rapids: Zondervan, 2000.

Managing Money

Alcorn, Randy. *The Treasure Principle: Unlocking the Secret of Joyful Giving.* LifeChange Books. Rev. ed. Sisters, OR: Multnomah, 2005.

Crown Financial Ministries. www.crown.org.

Morris, Robert. *The Blessed Life: The Simple Secret of Achieving Guaranteed Financial Results.* Ventura, CA: Regal, 2004.

Ramsey, Dave. *The Total Money Makeover: A Proven Plan for Financial Fitness.* 3rd ed. Nashville: Thomas Nelson, 2009.

Creating a Culture of Beauty

Creative Homeowner Editors. *The Smart Approach to Home Decorating.* 3rd ed. Creative Homeowner, 2007.

Gaither, Gloria, and Shirley Dobson. *Let's Make a Memory.* Rev. ed. Nashville: Thomas Nelson, 1994.

Sande, Ken, with Tom Raabe. *Peacemaking for Families: A Biblical Guide to Managing Conflict in Your Home.* Focus on the Family. Carol Stream, IL: Tyndale, 2002.

Professionalizing the Roles of Wife and Mother

Coroy, Carla Anne. *Married Mom, Solo Parent: Finding God's Strength to Face the Challenge.* Grand Rapids: Kregel, 2011.

Omartian, Stormie. *The Power of a Praying® Parent.* Eugene, OR: Harvest House, 1995.

Savage, Jill. *My Heart's at Home: Becoming the Intentional Mom Your Family Needs.* Eugene, OR: Harvest House, 2007.

Savage, Jill. *Professionalizing Motherhood: Encouraging, Educating, and Equipping Mothers At Home.* Grand Rapids: Zondervan, 2001.

Watters, Steve, and Candice Watters. *Start Your Family: Inspiration for Having Babies.* Chicago: Moody, 2009.

Choosing God's Best

Farrar, Mary. *Choices: For Women Who Long to Discover Life's Best.* Sisters, OR: Multnomah, 1994.

Kendrick, Stephen, and Alex Kendrick. *The Love Dare.* Nashville: B&H, 2008.

Lewis, Robert. *The New Eve.* Nashville: B&H, 2008.

Notes

Chapter 1: Equipping for the Journey

1. "Ruth Bell Graham: 1920–2007," Obituary, Billy Graham Evangelistic Association, June 14, 2007, http://www.billygraham.org/specialsections/rbg/RBG_Obituary.asp.

2. Earl Fluker and Catherine Tumber, *Strange Freedom: The Best of Howard Thurman on Religious Experience and Public Life* (Boston: Beacon, 1998), 100.

3. Ruth Bell Graham, "With Thanksgiving," *Decision Magazine*, Billy Graham Evangelistic Association, November 1, 2006, http://www.billygraham.org/articlepage.asp?articleid=746.

4. Robert Lewis with Jeremy Howard, *The New Eve* (Nashville: B&H, 2008), 43.

5. "Ruth Bell Graham: 1920–2007," Memories, Billy Graham Evangelistic Association, http://www.billygraham.org/specialsections/rbg/RBG_Memories.asp.

6. Willard F. Harley Jr., *His Needs, Her Needs*, 15th anniversary edition (Grand Rapids: Revell, 2001), 82.

7. Lewis, *New Eve*, 170–71.

8. Jennifer McBride, "Zig Ziglar: Embracing the Struggle," *Dallas Fort Worth Christian Family*, January 2011. http://www.dfwchristianfamily.com/cover/Zig-Ziglar.php.

9. Stormie Omartian, *The Power of a Praying® Wife* (Eugene, OR: Harvest House, 1997), 13. Used by permission.

Chapter 2: Attending to Self-Care

1. Joyce Meyer, *The Everyday Life Bible* (New York: FaithWords, 2006), 993.

2. Quoted by Amy M. Tatum, "Discovering a Healthier You," *Today's*

Christian Woman, September/October 2002, www.christianitytoday.com /tcw/2002/sepoct/8.76.html.

3. See www.walkathome.com.

4. Dr. Don Colbert, MD, "The Seven Pillars of Health," Resurrection Life Church, Grand Rapids, MI, May 19, 2007.

5. Quoted by Robert Barnett, "How to Be a Happier Mom," *Parenting Magazine,* January 2007, www.parenting.com/Common/printArticle .jsp?articleID=21334722.

Chapter 3: Living as the Genuine Article

1. John Eldredge and Stasi Eldredge, *Captivating: Unveiling the Mystery of a Woman's Soul* (Nashville: Thomas Nelson, 2005), 216.

2. Randy Alcorn, *The Treasure Principle: Unlocking the Secret of Joyful Giving,* rev. ed. (Sisters, OR: Multnomah, 2005), 75.

3. Ibid., 58.

4. William P. Young, *The Shack* (Newbury Park, CA: Windblown Media, 2007), 126.

5. Oswald Chambers, *My Utmost for His Highest,* ©1935 by Dodd Mead & Co., renewed ©1963 by the Oswald Chambers Publications Assn., Ltd. Used by permission of Discovery House Publishers, Grand Rapids, MI 49501.

Chapter 4: Cultivating Mystique

1. *Merriam-Webster's Collegiate Dictionary,* 11th ed., s.v. "mystique."

2. Dr. James Dobson, *Focus on the Family* radio broadcast, Colorado Springs, CO: 1986.

3. Jill Kreiger Swanson, *Simply Beautiful—Inside and Out* (Siren, WI: River City, 2005), 2.

4. Shaunti Feldhahn, *For Women Only: What You Need to Know About the Inner Lives of Men* (Sisters, OR: Multnomah, 2004), 165.

5. Ibid., 161.

6. *What a Girl Wants,* DVD, directed by Dennie Gordon (Warner Brothers, 2003).

7. *Merriam-Webster's,* s.v. "discretion."

8. See, for example, Joyce Meyer, "Do It Afraid!" Joyce Meyer Ministries, October 7, 2008, http://www.joycemeyer.org/Articles/ea.aspx?article=do _it_afraid.

9. Franklin D. Roosevelt, Inaugural Address (March 4, 1933).

Chapter 5: Inviting Romance

1. Richard T. Ritenbaugh, *Forerunner Commentary*, s.v. "Desire for Husband, Woman's," www.biblctools.org.

2. Edwin Louis Cole, *Absolute Answers to Prodigal Problems* (Southlake, TX: Watercolor, 2003), 35.

3. Jan Meyers, *The Allure of Hope: God's Pursuit of a Woman's Heart* (Colorado Springs: NavPress, 2001), 42.

Chapter 6: Thinking Differently About Sex

1. Linda Dillow and Lorraine Pintus, *Intimate Issues,* ©1999 by Linda Dillow and Lorraine Pintus. WaterBrook Press, Colorado Springs. Used by permission. All rights reserved.

2. "The Future of the Global Muslim Population: Projections for 2010–2030," Pew Forum, January 27, 2011, http://www.pewforum.org/The-Future-of-the-Global-Muslim-Population.aspx.

3. Paula Rinehart, *Sex and the Soul of a Woman* (Grand Rapids: Zondervan, 2004), 90, 92–93.

4. Ibid., 92.

5. Ibid., 102.

6. Shaunti Feldhahn, *For Women Only* (Sisters: Multnomah, 2004), 91.

7. Ibid., 93–94; emphasis in original.

8. Ibid., 104.

9. Ibid., 99.

10. Ibid., 101.

11. Ibid., 100.

12. Ibid., 96–97.

13. "Increase Your Low Libidio," Boston Medical Group, http://www.bostonmedicalgroup.com/ed/increase-libido (accessed November 23, 2011).

14. Feldhahn, *For Women Only,* 157; emphasis mine.

15. Laura Schlessinger, *The Proper Care and Feeding of Husbands* (New York: Harper Collins, 2006), 124.

16. Dillow and Pintus, *Intimate Issues*, 60.

17. Ibid., 59.

18. Stormie Omartian, *The Power of a Praying® Wife* (Eugene, OR: Harvest House, 2007), 61. Used by permission.

19. Ibid., 62.

20. Kevin Leman, *Sheet Music* (Wheaton: Tyndale, 2003), 184.

21. Ibid., 185.

22. Archibald Hart, *Adrenaline and Stress: The Exciting New Breakthrough That Helps You Overcome Stress Damage* (Nashville: Thomas Nelson, 1995), 83.

23. Ginny Graves, "Too Stressed for Sex?" *Ladies' Home Journal* (November 2004), http://www.lhj.com/health/sexual/sex/too-stressed-for-sex/.

Chapter 7: Opening Lines of Communication

1. "Delighting in Your Spouse's Differences 2," *Focus on the Family* broadcast, January 8, 2008; discussing the book *Men Are Like Waffles, Women Are Like Spaghetti* by Pam and Bill Farrel (Eugene, OR: Harvest House, 2001).

2. Tim Atkinson, "Imago Dialogue 101," Imago Relationships website, http://gettingtheloveyouwant.com/articles/imago-dialogue-101; copyright Helen LaKelly Hunt, Harville Hendrix, and Imago Relationships International 2007–2008. Imago therapy does not have a biblical basis, but as far as communication in relationships goes, the advice is sound. As with everything, bathe your communication in prayer and stay focused in God's Word.

Chapter 8: Speaking Truth in Love

1. Hannah Hurnard, *Hinds' Feet on High Places* (Carol Stream, IL: Tyndale, 1975), 66–67.

2. For your own copy of "Who I Am in Christ," see www.ficm.org /whoiam.htm, or call Freedom in Christ Ministries at (866) 462-4747.

3. Max Lucado, *A Love Worth Giving* (Nashville: Thomas Nelson, 2002), 6–7.

4. *Merriam-Webster's Collegiate Dictionary,* 11th ed., s.v. "passive."

5. Ibid., s.v. "aggressive."

6. Ruth N. Koch and Kenneth C. Haugk, *Speaking the Truth in Love: How to Be an Assertive Christian* (St. Louis: Stephen Ministries, 1992), 22. (Available online at www.stephenministries.com.)

7. Ibid.

8. Hurnard, *Hinds' Feet,* 238, 241–42.

Chapter 9: Managing Money

1. Suze Orman, *The 9 Steps to Financial Freedom* (New York: Three Rivers, 2006), 9.

2. Robert Morris, *The Blessed Life* (Ventura, CA: Regal, 2004), 29–30.

3. Randy Alcorn, *The Treasure Principle: Unlocking the Secret of Joyful Giving,* rev. ed. (Sisters, OR: Multnomah, 2005).

4. Ibid., 71.

5. Rick Warren, "Rick Warren's Second Reformation," interview by David Kuo, Beliefnet, www.beliefnet.com/Faiths/Christianity/2005/10 /Rick-Warrens-Second-Reformation.aspx (no date; accessed November 7, 2011).

6. American Bankruptcy Institute, "Annual and Quarterly U.S. Bankruptcy Statistics," www.abiworld.org/am/template.cfm?section=Bankruptcy _Statistics1 (no date; accessed November 8, 2011).

7. Mary Hunt, "Mary's Story," Debt-Proof Living, http://debtproofliving .com/MeetMary/MarysStory/tabid/212/Default.aspx (no date; accessed November 8, 2011).

8. From Katrina Baker, "Surviving the Splurge," *Today's Christian Woman,* January/February 2003. Used by permission.

9. "Fast Facts: The Faces of Poverty," Millennium Project (commissioned by the UN secretary general), 2002–2006, www.unmillenniumproject.org /resources/fastfacts_e.htm (no date; accessed November 8, 2011).

10. Dave Ramsey, "Nerds and Free Spirits Can Unite Over the Budget," daveramsey.com, January 18, 2010, http://www.daveramsey.com/article /nerds-and-free-spirits-can-unite-over-the-budget/lifeandmoney_budgeting

11. See, e.g., ibid.

Chapter 10: Creating a Culture of Beauty

1. Chris Casson Madden, "Decorating Can be Adventurous, Romantic or Serene," *Grand Rapids Press,* January 16, 2005.

2. Laurie Smith, *Guideposts,* September 2003.

3. "What Would Happen If Peace Really Ruled Your Life? Isn't It Time for Change?" Joyce Meyer Ministries newsletter, November 2007.

4. Mary Farrar, *Choices: For Women Who Long to Discover Life's Best* (Sisters, OR: Multnomah, 1994), 224.

5. Jeanie Lerche Davis, "Family Dinners Are Important: 10 Reasons Why, and 10 Shortcuts to Help Get the Family to the Table," WebMD, July 17, 2007, http://children.webmd.com/guide/family-dinners-are-important.

Chapter 11: Professionalizing the Roles of Wife and Mother

1. Gary Thomas, *Sacred Parenting: How Raising Children Shapes Our Souls* (Grand Rapids: Zondervan, 2005), 17.

2. Robert Lewis with Jeremy Howard, *The New Eve* (Nashville: B&H, 2008), 71.

3. Ibid.

4. G. K. Chesterton, "The Emancipation of Domesticity" from *What's Wrong with the World* (available via Project Gutenberg at www.gutenberg.org/ebooks/1717).

5. Matthew Henry, *Complete Commentary on the Whole Bible* (1706), http://www.sacred-texts.com/bib/cmt/henry/psa133.htm.

6. Vince Vaughn, "Trusting God in Times of Decision" (sermon, Buffalo Covenant Church, Buffalo, MN, August 2006).

7. Thomas, *Sacred Parenting,* 15.

8. Star Parker, "A Man Worth Listening To," *Grand Rapids Press,* December 30, 2007.

Chapter 12: Choosing God's Best

1. Robert Lewis with Jeremy Howard, *The New Eve* (Nashville: B&H, 2008), 11.

ABOUT SANDY RALYA AND
BEAUTIFUL WOMANHOOD

Sandy Ralya is the founder and director of Beautiful Womanhood and speaks to hundreds of women each year at MOPS groups, women's retreats, and church leadership conferences around the world. Beautiful Womanhood was born from Sandy's personal experience and conviction that mentoring helps women focus on God so they can experience greater fulfillment in marriage.

> "Focusing on God and sharing within a loving community of women has helped me grow my marriage—through all its ups and downs. This growth has awarded me strength and dignity and blessed my husband in countless ways." —*Sandy*

Since 2003, women have been coming together through Beautiful Womanhood small groups, where they gain insight from Sandy Ralya's teaching, personal guidance from a marriage mentor, and support from a loving community of women in order to grow as a wife.

Sandy and her husband, Tom, have been married since 1980 and have three adult children and a growing number of grandchildren. When not writing, Sandy enjoys shopping at yard sales for vintage clothing, cooking, traveling, and drinking really good coffee (black is best) with her husband. Sandy bases her ministry near Grand Rapids, Michigan.

Learn more about Beautiful Womanhood at
www.beautifulwomanhood.com.

Further focus and fulfillment for you, for your small group*, or for marriages you mentor

PRAYER JOURNAL

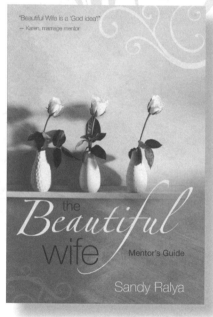

MENTOR'S GUIDE